PARENTS AS PLAYMATES

Joan Millman
Polly Behrmann

PARENTS AS PLAYMATES

Illustrations by
Dana B. Larrabee

HUMAN SCIENCES PRESS
72 Fifth Avenue   3 Henrietta Street
NEW YORK, NY 10011 ● LONDON, WC2E 8LU

Printed in the United States of America
  123456789 98765432

Library of Congress Cataloging in Publication Data

Millman, Joan.
    Parents as playmates.

    1. Educational games.   2. Education, Preschool.
3. Play.   I. Behrmann, Polly, joint author.   II. Title.
LB1137.M47   372.1'3   LC 79-4547
ISBN 0-87705-404-5

CONTENTS

PARENTS AS PLAYMATES

INTRODUCTION

How brief are the preschool years, marked by a child's boundless curiosity and a parent's limited time. Our little one looks at ivy and says, "*Why* are we growing leaves on the house?" He shouts, "*Why* do I have to be quiet?" when someone is asleep. The child is long on energy and short in attention; while we may be high on expectations and low in patience. Children want to know the why of all sorts of things but can't see the why of dressing or sitting still or not touching or being quiet in hushed places.

We have raised eight children between us, and we remember—oh, how we remember—those endless days of rain; those worrisome, sick-in-bed times; those harried moments of squeezing twenty-four hours into twelve; the chaos of everything-going-wrong; and worst of all, days when we were too ill to cope. We have known the cabin fever of long winters. We remember having company and being it; the daytrips, not bad if well planned, and the long trips, a disaster when the unplanned occurred. Our children fought with each other and made up before we figured out appropriate solutions. We went to bed at night wondering if we had done *anything* right.

Now our "terrible two's" have grown, some to teenage; some beyond, and not only have we survived, but hopefully they survived having us.

The purpose of this is to help parents and preschoolers come together in a relaxed yet meaningful manner. Of course, when we are tired, busy, or out-of-sorts, it is easy to say "don't!" or "no!" We all do it. Turning ticklish times into enriching ones takes a little more imagination. We hope that the ideas contained here can serve as guidelines, and we will talk to both parents and preschoolers.

For instance, we don't believe parents should take their children everywhere. Indeed we encourage time away from them. But we do believe family outings ought to be pleasant for *both* adults and children. We offer games as a "sugar-coated" way to spark any circumstance. Play often leads to learning; we from our children as well as they from us. Be open. Let your child lead you into his or her special world.

The situations here are all natural ones: bedtimes, bathtimes, beachtimes, playgrounds and picnics, doctors' offices and waiting rooms. The settings are in the kitchen, car, or restaurant; on rainy, sick, or any ordinary day. When time hangs, we fill it with "toys": common objects found in a purse or pocket, the signs on the walls, silverware on a table.

While the activities are primarily fun, they can be educational. Listening to a birdsong develops auditory acuity, a skill needed for distinguishing letter sounds in reading or spelling. Counting people on a bus lays the groundwork for basic math. The materials are everywhere: newspapers, cartons, magazines, buttons, playing cards, plastic containers, bowls, shoelaces, marbles. Why can't a puppet be fashioned from a pipecleaner or a discarded sock? Or a turkey baster be a tub toy?

Early childhood may seem forever, but it is so terribly short. It can be the most rewarding time for everyone in the family, the basis for a good relationship in later years. And just when the family has actually survived this period, then the child's stubborn, independent, and venturesome nature comes back like a relapse when—oh no—he is a teen.

LANGUAGE DEVELOPMENT

What more natural bond is there between people than talk? Even a newborn responds to the human voice and learns early its importance in communication. A rich listening environment is a treasure any adult can give a little one. Since understanding speech comes before the child is able to speak, any time is the right time to talk to the baby. While dressing him, say softly, "Here is a blue nightie. Now I am wrapping you in your warm blanket. Soon you'll be tucked in snugly."

Descriptive words such as adjectives, adverbs, and action verbs spice a listening experience. We like variety in what we eat. Language, too, can be a feast of words. To a toddler, for example, we say, "Here is a glass of orange juice." On another day we could phrase it this way, "Here is a tumbler of orange juice." (To say nothing of those days when it is a *tumble* of orange juice!)

Young children often lack the understanding of spatial concepts of above, below, left, right, inside, over, under. While tucking her in, you might say, "Jane is under the blanket." Or help Susy "put the toys inside the toy box." While setting the table, why not point out, "Here are the forks on the left, the spoons on the right."

Meal times are social as well as functional and are the ideal opportunity for family conversation. A parent should say, "Please pass the rolls," rather than nodding or pointing to them. When a child is asked if he wants seconds, he should be encouraged not merely to nod or grunt an answer. This is not a prejudice for good manners; it is a guide to good speech.

The dinner table is when a child may be invited to "tell his day." Even a simple reply deserves attention. We hope you will not judge your child on the sophistication of his or her speech. Perhaps a neighbor's child talks "like a professor" while yours still lisps or mispronounces *l*'s or *r*'s. Speech, like every other skill, matures at different rates.

While sometimes in our busy lives we let a child's question go unanswered, we are also guilty of occasionally giving *too* much answer, which only turns off communication.

Let the dialogue in the book serve merely as examples. No two children speak alike. Enjoy your child's unique style of communication. It is sometimes poetry.

WALKS

Children thrive on routine. A daily walk gives a security of companionship and is especially recommended for adults who have little time to spend with children. It has the advantage, as well, of increasing adult energy while wearing out the child, which makes for a delightful contrast. Walks are for seeing, sharing, talking, and growing in many ways.

Establish the habit in every kind of weather, pointing out the appropriate clothing for the day.

If the walk is at the same time every day, observe the position of the sun. Tie this into the changing seasons.

Begin with a short walk to a specific destination. Try to lengthen the distance every time. Both walkers can have the satisfaction of building stamina this way.

Social Interactions

Walks are times to *teach* about fire hydrants, telephone poles, electric wires, crosswalks, catch-basins.

Walks are times to *caution* about strange dogs, talking to strangers, crossing when the lights are red.

Walks are times to *study* air and water pollution, litter, cleanliness, junk foods at quick take-out spots.

Walks are times to *talk* about people, the different colored packaging they come in, called skin.

Walks are times to *watch* at what speeds different vehicles move, how animals move, how birds fly, how worms wiggle, and how insects buzz about.

Walks are time to *wonder* about revolving doors, flags going up on poles, fire engine sirens, water gushing down drainpipes, and seeping into sewers.

Walks are times to *observe* the variety of vegetables at the market, the flowers in gardens, the assortment of building materials, statues in the park.

Walks are times to *get acquainted* with the new couple on the street, the widow down the hall, other children in the playground, the policeman or woman directing traffic.

Walks in the rain are a time to *count* the different colors of umbrellas, to *jump* over puddles, to be *glad* all of nature is getting a drink.

Walks in the snow are a time to *reflect* on what makes winter a wonderland and why it is different from any other time of year.

Body Movements   Ask the child how many kinds of body movements can he make. Can he balance on a low wall, twirl in a field (but don't get dizzy), jump, dance, sway, swing, leap, run, prance, skip, turn somersaults, cartwheels, handstands, crawl or creep in tall grass, and whatever you do, call out the name of the action and stretch vocabulary as well as muscles.

Kaleidoscope   Nature's variety is to be savored. Pay special attention to her tints and shades and hues. Sunsets and moon rises and star twinkles and even the drabness of a storm-coming sky. How many black things are there and are they all the same degree of black? Gray? Blue? Green?

Games for Walking   *Walk on a Crack, Break Your Mother's Back*—Try to skip over the lines on a sidewalk.

Walking Backwards—Good for walks in grassy fields; challenging for little ones.

Counting Steps—How many to the telephone pole, to the store, to the barn door?

Strides   Taking long strides and short ones, quick or slow, jogging together, pacing yourselves, make it fun to be on a walk. Watch others on the street. Do they take long strides, walk in mincing steps, lumber, stroll, or rush? How do animals get where they are going? Everything from a gallop to a bunny hop.

Singing   Walking and singing are comrades.

Marching songs and marching feet

Happy ditties and dancing feet

Sing-a-longs and skip-a-long feet

Harmonicas, homemade drums, kazoos, flags, ribbons, anything to beat or swing to keep pace with the rhythm of walking.

Imitative Play   Can you walk like a cowboy or like a soldier? Tiptoe like a ballet dancer or a bareback rider in a circus? Can you be a tired old person or waddle like a duck? How does a queen walk toward her throne, or how does a sailor walk on a rocking ship?

Ecology   Take a large plastic bag along to pick up scraps of paper. Do the world a favor!

Sizes   Compare: big house, little house; big dog, little dog; fat man, thin man; tall pole, short pole; long line, short line; wide road, narrow road.

Shapes   Find objects that are circles: pools, tires, clocks, manhole covers, traffic lights; then find squares, diamonds, triangles, and rectangles on subsequent days. Distinguishing shapes is the beginning of seeing the difference in numbers and letters.

Counting   Count how many hydrants, mailboxes, and traffic lights you come across. See if you can find 10 or 20 of a given object. See if there are "more" or "less" of a given object on a particular day, as compared to yesterday. Occasionally carry a pad of paper and keep score.

Letters   Can the child spot a sign with the first initial in his name during the walk? A very sophisticated skill would be to spot letters in alphabetical order (not usually accomplished in the preschool years).

Ted: I see an "A" in that gas station sign.

Roger: There's a "B" in the store window.

Carol: Shucks, I don't see a "C" anywhere.

(Wait till you need a J, X, or Z!)

Before and After   The sequence of events is an extremely difficult concept for young children to grasp. Where there were trees, there is suddenly a building. Where there was only a foundation, there eventually becomes a house. Unless you can observe these developments at close hand, perhaps on a daily basis, there is a sense of the "unreal" about much that is done around and above a small child.

> Dad: Looks like they got that big hole dug today after all. We saw all that heavy construction machinery *yesterday.*
>
> Bobby: What're they gonna do with the hole? Can I dig in it?
>
> Dad: Well, son, looks like they must be getting ready to build a really big building. That sure is a big hole.
>
> Bobby: When?
>
> Dad: When we come back here *tomorrow* we'll be able to see if they have begun to put in the foundation. That is to a building, Bobby, what your feet are to you.

The Person of Trees   Just as each person walks, moves, and has a distinguishing characteristic of his own, so do trees. Point out the tall and regal, the broad and squat, the grace of boughs easily bent, the sway of laden branches, the upreach to the sky of another, and if possible the fruit tree heavy with its "cargo." Observe the silhouette of trees against the dusk or the night. Do they look different in different light, in different seasons? Some families select a favorite tree to visit and observe on a regular basis. Or, if possible, plant one for each member of the family and keep records of the growth and development of each person's tree. The whisper of branches against a house at night or in a storm can be a welcome, friendly sound to a child.

Travel Buddies   Some children will carry their security blanket or favorite stuffed animal or doll on a walk. All sorts of things lend themselves to the child who likes to carry something along:

- Balloons on a string
- Beanbags to toss back and forth with a walking partner
- Batons to twirl

- Ribbons to wave gayly

- Toys to pull or push

- A friend

A favorite book for children throughout the world is the French story *The Red Balloon*. It depicts the fantasy experience of a small boy who is walking with a balloon on the streets of Paris, and should be as much a part of a child's picture-story experience as any other classic.

Sounds

Listen to all that can be heard!

City Sounds.   Engines, exhausts, ambulances, footsteps, voices, cries, laughs, whistles, horns, doors banging, pipes clanging, jack hammers drumming, brakes squeaking. What can you hear? Can you close your eyes and guess what is making the sound? Can you tell what is far and what is near?

Country Sounds.   Birds singing, cows mooing, chickens clucking, branches swishing, horses clopping, dogs barking, or a voice calling the cows home.

Apartment Buildings.   Doors closing, people talking or shouting, telephones ringing, records playing, instruments being practiced, footsteps on the stairs.

Parks.   Children playing, talking from transistor radios, dogs barking, and noises of games. Try and close your eyes and guess what game is being played.

Smells

Train your nose to make your walk richer. Stop when you pass the gas station and sniff in its special smell. Explore the scent of a construction site, the smell of men at work and machinery blended in. Smell a newly-cut lawn or field of hay. Smell the must of a bog or the moss around an old tree. A bus emits a powerful odor from its exhaust (danger!) and burning leaves emit a whispy smell.

The child was so tantalized by the aroma eminating from a nearby bakery that he let go of his mom's hand and quietly slipped inside. Before he was noticed or missed, he had begun to eat the cookies fresh from the oven and on display.

Touches

"Don't touch" is too often the case for little children, but important learning begins at the fingertips. When texture has been explored, the character of an object has greater meaning to a child. Instruct from the earliest age what is "touchable" and what is not. A child must begin to realize that some objects are too sharp, hot, prickly, or threatening to be approached. To offset these limits, encourage touching wherever possible.

Find objects that are sandy, mottled, rough, brushy, splintery, metallic, furry, grainy, gritty, pebbly, rocky, cold, smooth, and slippery. The child will have colorful words for the feel of things as well.

Aesthetics

Ask your child to try to describe his own feelings: How do you feel when you walk past a beautiful garden? How does it feel to watch the sun go down? What do you think about when you see so many people hurrying home? What does it make you feel like to stretch your neck to look up to the top of the highest building? What are you thinking when you look down at that tiny ant burdened with food for her family?

Who Does What?

A preschooler is totally ignorant of the variety of careers men and women pursue. It is often hard to understand what one's own parents do on their jobs, unless it is a job that is clearly visible to a child. On a walk, look for a person with an apron who may be stacking vegetables in the market or tossing pizzas in the restaurant window or cutting cold cuts for lunch tomorrow. (Why cold cuts? Are there hot cuts?)

Notice the person wearing a charcoal gray uniform with a bird on his or her hat, driving a red, white, and blue truck. The truck has the same colors as the flag. We all know the postman or woman, but have we observed the details of their uniform?

There is the man with his shirt off. He is a construction worker and he works so hard, he gets hot and sweaty, and feels more comfortable without his top. But he always wears a hard hat. (Why a hard hat? Is there a soft hat?)

Why do nurses and barbers wear white? And why do barber poles have red and white stripes?

Exotic Objects Aside from their fascinating functions, many objects have fascinating names: fire escape, skyscraper ("skyscratcher" to some) jack hammer, moving van, vending machine, turnstile, subway stop.

A three year old put himself to sleep at naptimes by sing songing the rhythms of words he liked. Sometimes he droned the names of his friends, like a roll call. Other times he repeated over and over a particularly rich phrase: skyscraper, skyscraper, skyscraper, until he was fast asleep.

Solo Flight And then the day comes when taking a walk means taking it by oneself. The child is ready to leave the nest at least for a little while and a little distance. One mother recalls that day as though it were yesterday, even though that little one is now grown and married. First she analyzed his sense of responsibility. Would he look carefully both ways while crossing the street? (It was in a suburban neighborhood selected for its safety and lack of daytime traffic.) Would he walk only on the "sidewalk"? (The only sidewalks were grassy separations between the road and the yards.) Would he treat each driveway as though it were a major highway? (You never knew when a car would suddenly bomb out of a garage.) And when he got there (which was two blocks away) would he call at once to assure her he was okay?

The child nodded a solemn yes to all of these questions. Surely he felt like he was setting out on a dangerous mission. To his mother, he gave his pledge of maturity and responsibility.

Still the mother worried. He had never played out of the yard, and was always within her easy supervision. So she checked up on him by calling neighbors along the boy's route. Was he following instructions? "Yes," the wiser mothers smiled on the phone. "Don't worry, he's walking very carefully and very proudly." For a three year old, he was extremely *responsible.*

Then the mother knew the apron strings had been cut and that the little boy would soon belong to the world.

GETTING THERE

For many people, it is the "there" that is important and the "getting" that is an ordeal. Some children come running to a car key jingle. Others sleep peacefully through an entire trip, a motor as good as a lullabye. And then there are others so active in any confined place that even short outings are resentfully deferred by the parents. Whether or not your child is a "natural" traveler, planning ahead can increase the pleasure and lessen the pain.

Attire   While traveling, "best" clothes are usually in order. But is that the most comfortable way to travel? Why not dress the youngster in broken-in ones en route and make a last minute change?

Shoes start off shiny and end up scuffed; barefeet (in mild weather) during the trip can give a child more "breathing" space. When a child must not only "sit still" for safety's sake, but stay clean and pressed, everyone's mood becomes as tattered as the clothing.

Rare is the child who will stay clean even on short auto trips. If a clean face and hands match the event (i.e. church, family party), keep commercially-dampened paper products on hand. If you are merely going where the tot will only get dirtier (playground, parade, amusement park), why fuss? The tub later is a better place to tend to hygiene.

Always bring a sweater for warmth, underwear for accidents.

The Worries   When a child is worried about the unknown, it is usually based on what is already known. Past experience may have made the new experience less than a happy one. Did parent and child become separated at the zoo? Did the little one feel swept away by the crowd streaming onto the ferry? Was there no nearby toilet facility and was the tramp in the woods too far from a drinking fountain? A child cannot always express the reason for balking at what an adult assures will be "fun."

The little girl bubbled along, her hand tucked solidly in daddy's. She chattered about the roller coaster, the target games, the stuffed prizes. The "daddy" was too tall for her to realize he was the wrong "daddy," and the strange man was too tactful to interrupt his sudden new charge. All at once the genuine Daddy rushed up and grabbed his little girl, awakening her to her embarrassment.

"Oh Daddy," she cried, as she happily hugged the real McCoy. "I thought he was you!"

Pretrip Tips

An ounce of preparation is most important before any trip. Store ahead a few inexpensive items, such as pipe cleaners. Buy a different color for each child to avoid the "it's mine, no, it's mine" background music. These are quiet, safe, unbreakable, and lend themselves to numerous variations: letters C D P, puppets bent into "hang-man shapes,"   rings and bracelets. They can be counted, stacked, sorted, traded, woven. A glove-compartment is a handy place to keep them between trips.

Say It With Pictures

Reassure timid children with much preparation and description of the new experience. Magazine pictures or library books that feature the zoo, museum, aquarium, etc., are good to orient a child. Encourage conversation while examining the pictures. Don't be surprised at the preconceived ideas some children have about an unknown place! Familiarity engenders security.

The "worldly" two-year old had been exposed to all the local cultural opportunities. As he was once again being bundled into best clothes, he sighed, "Oh another zoo-seum, huh?"

Truck Freaks

Some children are obsessed with toy vehicles, spending endless hours in sandbox construction. Such little ones can take along a bag full of small plastic cars and trucks. Assorted vehicles are best, for the child can then be on the lookout for matching ones on the highway. Permit imaginative play on the backseat of a car, or, when possible, select the large rear seat of a bus or subway.

Mind Stretchers

Objects taken for granted by adults are often fascinating and new to young children. While riding, the child will notice telephone wires and suspension bridges whizzing past, overhead luggage racks, bus tickets stuck in the back of the seat ahead, drop-down trays on a plane and so on. The questions will fly as fast as the vehicle and the "don't touches" abound. Expect and *encourage* a child's curiosity.

Grandpa: Ever see a paper punch, Ronnie? Watch now, the conductor is going to come down the aisle and punch a hole in every ticket.

Ronnie: How come?

Grandpa: That's to know where each passenger is going. There is a word on the ticket for each bus stop.

Ronnie: What's a passenger?

I Spy Talking about all the new wonders makes the time fly on a trip.
"I spy something puffy with straps and a buckle above a seat."
"Is it a suitcase?"
"Yes, it is on a luggage rack because a suitcase is also called luggage."

Time, Sequence, and Speed

Time is a most elusive concept to a child, and often a lifetime problem for people who are always late. "A little while," "soon," "not long," what do these phrases mean to a child? Whenever possible use a tangible method to lessen travel anxiety. Large simple clocks and watches for a child to observe the hands' passage, oven timers, the dropping numbers on a car's speedometer, the computerized TV screen in an airport reporting arrivals and departures, all of these teach a child rules and routines. There is nothing magic about distance, length, speed, and duration, even if they seem as mysterious to a child as time itself.

Time. Try to associate time segments with a familiar period.

Jeannie: (whining) "How long, how much *longer* to Grandma's?"

Sis: (sighing) "Two hours, hon. Do try to be patient!"

Jeannie: "Two hours!" (close to tears).

Sis: "Well, that's how long you watch cartoons on Saturday morning."

Jeannie: "Oh is that all two hours is? That's only a little!"

Sequence.   Small children have difficulty understanding "last week" or "next month." So much of life and learning depends on understanding the natural sequence of events (what is happening right now, what comes next, etc.) that an adult can automatically use these concepts in daily conversation. To give a travel-worried youngster additional security, alert him or her to the expected order of events.

Sam: What is there to do at Aunt Mary's? Will there be any kids?

Mother: First Aunt Mary will give us a hug. You know how glad she'll be to see us. Then she'll take us upstairs to our rooms and we can unpack. Then she'll probably have warm cookies from the oven, her yummy chippedy ones. *Then* I bet she'll have something special for you to play with.

Sam: Some*thing?*

Mother: Yes, in the basement. A brand new Collie pup!

Speed.   Simple concepts and contrasts can be grasped at this age. The mechanically-minded might even be interested in looking under a car hood for a simple lesson in "horsepower." Why is a motor measured in horses? Why do planes travel faster than trains? Do jets fly faster than the little plane that reports the traffic in big cities? A bike can only move as fast as its owner's "foot-power," and a sailboat must depend on the wind. This simple approach to transportation lays the groundwork for future lessons in more formal settings.

Copy Cats   As travel time stretches, travel space shrinks. Think of activities that do not require much physical movement. Occupy the little one with facial dramatics. (To be played by passengers only, never drivers!)

Mom: I will make a funny face. Can you copy it?

Timmy: Sure, how's this one (giggling)?

Mom: Now I'll make a sad face. How about you?

Mom: Good. Why do you suppose someone is sad? Can we make up a sad face story? How about an angry face story? Can you show me an angry body, too? Can you show me a sleepy one?

Memory Stretchers

It is good training for visual recall (later needed for reading and writing) to play memory games that require closing one's eyes and listing what one has seen. Begin by focusing on one object and then move on to general things.

Dad: Take a good look at Mom's clothes, Betsy, and close your eyes. I'll give you a raisin for each thing you can remember.

Betsy: Hmm, let me see. A dress, hat, jacket.

Dad: That's all? There's more raisins waiting for you.

Betsy: Let's see. Beads, gloves, boots.

Dad: Now, hon, let's play how many things you can remember in the car.

Betsy: The suitcase. The snacks. And oh, yes, Poochie!

Finger Plays

These are some of the most familiar finger plays:

- "Where is Thumbkin?"
- "One Potato, Two Potato."
- "Eensie, weensie, spider."
- "Here is the church, here is the steeple."
- "Johnny, Johnny, Johnny whoops, Johnny whoops, etc."
- "Alouette, gentil Alouette."
- "Two little blackbirds."
- "One, two, buckle my shoe."

Quik-Piks

"Can you make your head be a camera? Take a quick picture of something you can see and give me a hint." Expect the child to describe a single object or two. Try to guess what it is.

Sally: "Something very, very, tall with lots of windows."

Mom: "Is it the big new building ahead?"

Above and Below   Take advantage of boredom by focusing on things above, below, next to, on top of, and so on. Eye direction is an important preparation for reading. "Can you see something above the man in front of us?" "The light." "What has the lady put under her seat?" "Her suitcase." "What is beside the driver?" "The coin box."

Oral History   A child rarely tires of hearing about his or her earliest days. "When you were a brand new baby in the hospital, we wrapped you in a pink shawl that grandma made just for you." "Then what?" "Then the nurse handed you over for us to take you home, but first she teased us and said we couldn't have you because she wanted to keep you for herself." "How come?" "Because she said you were the best baby in the nursery." A little body contact, a hug, and a squeeze, make the story even warmer.

Nonsense   Nonsense tales develop imagination and a sense of humor.

"Once there was a bunny who went to school," the first storyteller begins. The next goes on, "Then she became so smart she made the teacher sit with the class so she could teach them." "But the principal was a mad old alligator," the story is continued. Let a round-robin story unfold with as much nonsense as you can muster.

Do not tell scary tales to small children.

What-If Stories   What if Goldilocks had not been frightened away from the three bears? What do you think she would have done?

What if the handsome prince had not come by to awaken Snow White? Or, what if Snow White's stepmother had been kind and loving? How do you think the story would go?

What if Jack had not chopped down the beanstalk? What if the beanstalk had not grown so high? What do you suppose would have happened to Jack and his mother?

Fantasy Stories   Stretch the imagination as far as it will go. How about a story of a mailbox that walks and talks; a chair that flies when you sit on it; a tree that dances with you;

a cloud that rains salty tears; an ocean that covers you with silver beads.

Let your child think of a fantasy and then you weave it into a story (if you can.)

Categories Pinpointing details is excellent visual training. Decide on a category and see how many of them you can find as the world flies past your window.

- Small foreign cars
- Motorcycles
- McDonalds' arches
- Traffic lights (red or green or yellow)

Scorecards. A pad of paper is handy to keep score of whatever object is being counted.

traffic lights	yellow	green	red
	1111	/	11
policemen	directing traffic		in a car
	̶7̶H̶H̶		/

Comparison Games
- If it is not high it is _____?
- If it is not cold it is _____?
- If it is not fat it is _____?
- If it is not old it is _____?

Travel Memories There are variations on travel books. A travel book can be created before a trip, to keep for a souvenir of the trip, or be put together later to help a child recall its highpoints.

Pretrip.   Collect suitable pictures, either from magazines or postcards, that depict some of the highlights of the coming trip. If farm animals will be seen on the way, make a scrapbook of these pictures together. If it is to be a city trip or one that will have a woodsy scene, appropriate pictures can be found to prepare the child. Later, the book can have a cover and date, and perhaps it will be the first of a lifelong travelog collection.

Post-trip.   Let the child collect any memorabilia, such as restaurant napkins or stirrers, pennants, postcards, bumper stickers, decals or buttons, for the purpose of making a travel scrapbook after the trip.

Talkabouts.   It is fun to reminisce at any age. After the trip try to recall with your child significant events in the order they took place. "First we stopped to fill the car with gas. Then we checked the tires. Then I was thirsty and had a drink."

It is also fun to try to see who in the family can remember the most of a given object. "At how many restaurants did we stop? How many new people did we meet? How many cousins came to see us at grandma's?"

All the preparations were made, the car was loaded and at last the family was on its way. The car groaned out of the driveway with a pair of parents relieved and satisfied that finally the trip had begun. When they had gone about a mile or so, the mother looked back to check the baby in the car bed, and lo and behold! They had remembered everything they had needed to take for the trip but the baby!

Emergency Flares

To avoid "flare-ups" here is a list of "emergency flares":

- Nausea bags (as airlines usually provide)

- Packaged clean-up tissues, both the prewet and dry

- Pot with tight lid for when the child can't "wait another minute"

- Extra clothing

- Small soft toys: dolls, puppets, stuffed animals (A hand that is holding something cannot sock a sibling or hang out the window.)

- Security blanket or pillow. One family scoured Radio City Music Hall in New York looking for Robin's lost "blankie."

- Drinking water. Kids are *always* thirsty.

No infant or child should ever be transported without the protection of a safety seat. The only safe situation for a small child or infant in an automobile is to be fastened into an approved, crash-tested, safety device or seat which has been installed properly. There are many which meet these standards. Some are for infants, others for children up to forty pounds and some can be converted as the infant grows. Cost varies from $25 to $40. (See leaflet entitled "Ride Right.")* Unfortunately, at the present time, standards established by the U.S. Government use a static test rather than crash testing with the result that many seats are approved which fail to pass more stringent crash situations. A device, therefore, tagged as meeting government standards may not provide adequate protection. Patents must limit their choices to seats listed as having passed under crash test conditions. Serious injury and even fatalities have been reported with automobiles moving as slowly as 12 miles per hour. Children easily become adapted to the seat especially if it is used from the first automobile ride. Most devices provide better vision for the youngster and the driver has the security of knowing the child's location in the car. Studies have shown that behavior is greatly improved when such devices are a routine part of automobile travel.

At the present time, relatively few small children are adequately protected. Some studies have placed usage at as low as 7% while others question selection of approved safety-tested devices and utilization in all riding situations. Since the automobile is practically an extension of the home to most American families, it is important that parents and all others caring for small children be aware of the importance of automobile safety devices. Children under four years of age and/or forty pounds in weight need special safety seats and cannot use the regular car seat belts. The relatively small cost of these devices is more than offset by the peace of mind gained by using them.

Field Trips The usual places to take children such as zoos, museums, parks, farms are not the only fascinating places for children to visit. Common errors adults make is expecting longer attention spans than little people can sustain. We observed one mother tell a two year old, "We'll begin here and work our way through the building." The child was tired before they even began. It is best to sample large places, tasting a little each time. Prepare a youngster by saying, "We'll look at all the stuffed birds and then go for ice cream," or "We'll stop and look at the animals that swim" and then plan to return to see some other aspect of the exhibit.

*Courtesy Mass. Public Health Dept.

Because children are blessed with curiosity about places most of us now take for granted, a "field trip" to a child may very well be some place as common as the neighborhood market or as near as the post office. They are usually fascinated by the origin of food, not knowing what is processed or natural; if it comes from the ground or a machine; if it is cooked, frozen, etc. Both boys and girls are intrigued with anything mechanical.

Here are some places that can be visited (Be sure to phone first for permission!):

Bakery.   Backstage at a bakery is the best of all places. Icing a cake is an artform. Prearrange your visit, and perhaps the baker will ice a cookie with your little one's name on it.

Fish Market.   A fish on ice is easier to examine than one wiggling on a hook. Such variety! Not only are they picturesque, but their names enrich a child's vocabulary: mackerel, pickerel, haddock, sole, scrod, bluefish (is it?), white fish (is it?), porgies, bass. Why are some fish called shellfish? Examine lobster and crab claws. How are they different from fingers?

Delicatessen.   The rows of smoked meat are like a still-life painting. But delis are not just for looking, they're for sniffing. Order small amounts of spicy and exotic treats to sample. This might be the beginning of a gourmet and the end of the "hamburger-only" diet most children prefer.

Gas Stations.   Let a little air from the pump blow on the legs. Why does the mechanic raise a car on an auto lift? Watch the numbers jingle on the gas pumps.

Police Station.   Learn that a policeman is a friend and can help a child who is lost. Your child worries about safety and health.

Post Office.   Study the WANTED men and women and their fingerprints.

Every afternoon after school the first grader made a stop before coming home. He liked to look in at the post office and check the pictures on the wall. How he hoped he would be able to identify one of the "wanted men" and win that big reward.

Hospital Emergency Room.   If there is a nearby hospital or clinic, do not wait for an emergency to orient your child to the mysteries of its care. Usually a child who is ill or who has suffered an accident is a frightened child. It helps if the emergency room is not another factor added to his or her fright.

Other people and places your child may be interested in are:

- Butchers

- Fire stations

- Town dumps

- Library (the sorting and cataloging process)

- Dairy

- Telephone company

- Department of Public Works (especially the heavy construction and street-cleaning equipment)

- Tree warden and/or nursery

- Dog pound

- Humane society

- Newspaper plant

- Printers

- Candle factory

- Candy factory

- Craftsmen's studios

- Factories of any kind

The steel plant had an arrow painted on its floor for children to walk on while taking a tour of the facilities. One young child was so intrigued by keeping his feet on the arrow, he forgot to look up at the plant.

QUIET TIMES

There are short periods of quiet time that lend themselves to meaningful child–adult interaction. Relationships are built not so much on the quantity of time spent together, as the quality of it.

Resting-times, just-before-bedtimes, taking-a-bath-times, waiting-for-others-to-get-ready-times, getting-dressed-times, etc. These one-to-one activities build the moments to be remembered.

Bedtime Beginnings

What child willingly goes off to bed? Stories, simple games, songs, and poetry are soothing. Help the overactive youngster calm down, before tucking in. Records played when the lights go out prevent numerous poppings out of bed. Why fight "one more drink, one more kiss, one more stuffed toy"? Join it!

ROUTINES

Very young children derive security by establishing pre-bedtime routine. Perhaps it is placing one's slippers beside the bed, tucking in Teddy, a drink of water, a "nighty night" kiss for a pet or a member of the family. Repeat the schedule in order, nightly, and when all steps are completed, firmly say, "Good night!"

TALK-OUTS

Bedtime lends itself to casual discussion. Allow time for talking over what happened that day, and what is expected to happen next.

Mom: Elsa, it was nice of you to let Sam use your tricycle today when he came to visit. He rides it very well, doesn't he? He has such long legs, they reach the pedals more easily than yours do. Pretty soon, when you grow a little, you will ride better too. (Although Elsa has not said anything, Mother observed her "decision" not to ride any more.)

or

Mom: Tomorrow we must wake up a little earlier. We are going shopping, and I want to be at the stores before they get too crowded. (Elsa will not feel rushed in the morning if she is prepared.)

or

Dad: Son, that was very grown up of you to give me a hand this morning. I need all the help I can get when I clean the yard.

Chipper: Oh, gee, Dad, it was easy.

CALENDARS

A good calendar to use is the type that shows the month on a page, and that has boxes large enough to draw pictures in. Upcoming birthdays may be marked with child-drawn cakes. Suitable holidays may also be decorated in the boxes. When the child rises, let him color in blue for dark or rainy days, yellow for bright ones. At night, it is good routine to mark off that calendar day with an "X." In this way the children can see when Friday is, or Tuesday was.

CHARTS

A chart is a very visual way to encourage action. Giving checks or stars for good behavior helps a little one see what direction he or she is going in. The chart ought to be specific. If picking up one's clothes or toys, not spilling milk, or tieing shoelaces is what the parent is aiming for, only one of these goals should be indicated on the chart. Give a point every time the child remembers. No penalty is given for forgetting. Accentuate the positive! Of course, there will be backsliding. No one is perfect!

Nancy: Whoopee, I'm finally learning how to hang up my jacket when I come in. You didn't have to tell me once this week.

Mom: Good girl. Now how about a chart for putting your p.j.'s in the hamper?

Nancy: Aw, gee, Mom. Do I hafta? Couldn't I just be me for a while?

Mom: Okay, what do you say we don't have any more charts for a couple of weeks? And then we'll talk about it again. I'm very proud of you and this chart shows it.

PHENOMENA

In *summer*, bring a pair of fireflies into the house in a jar. In the dark room, let the child watch them flicker and glow. He'll find them fascinating!

In *winter*, place a bowl of water on a radiator at night. See how much has evaporated in the morning. Explain how "dry" the room is, and that water helps make the air "damp," a more comfortable way to sleep.

MOTHER GOOSE

Select the rhymes that are appropriate for bedtime.

"Wee Willie Winkie, running through the town; upstairs and downstairs in his nightgown."

"Jack-be-nimble, Jack-be-quick; Jack jump over the candlestick."

Can the nimble one jump over something and right into bed?

PICTURE BOOKS

A favorite that is read and reread, or a brand new library book, whatever you choose, a bedtime story is one of the best paths toward beautiful dreams.

LULLABIES

"Rock-a-bye Baby" to a doll or Teddy

"Bye, baby bunting, father's gone a-hunting . . ."

"Toora-Loora . . ."

"All through the night . . ."

Holding a child and quietly rocking him or her in your arms, and humming together is soothing for bedtime. Try Brahm's Lullaby. Lullabies do not have to have words.

Bathtime Warm baths before bed, both night-time and naptime, are soothing and help an active child unwind for sleep. Scrub-up time allows a parent to communicate in two ways: (1) playing educational games is instructional, and (2) the attention of body contact is emotionally nourishing. How one handles a little one, gently or impatiently, sets the tone of the relationship. It is better to skip the bath if the adult is rushing to get out, than to skip the "love-vitamins" bathtime gives a child.

LEARN ABOUT ME

Never underestimate a child's fascination with the human body. From infancy, a curious tot is busy exploring himself. In water, free of restricting clothing, he can fully examine all his parts. Help him learn about his body while washing each part.

"Here is Annie's little foot. My, how dirty this ankle is. How did your knees get so grubby? My, what a fat, round stomach. I can feel a hot dog and a soft drink when I pat it. Can you show me your elbow so I can make it clean? Can you make a fist, and show me your muscle?"

UNDERWATER

"Do your toes and fingers look different under water? Wiggle them and find out." What happens to the washcloth when it sinks beneath the water? Does it look the same as when it went in? Examine bathtoys above and under water. Do colors seem to change? Do they feel slippery? Can the child describe that feeling?

Preswim.   A child may begin his swimming lessons in the tub. He may blow bubbles and listen to the sound they make. "Close your eyes and put your head in the water" (when there is no soap). "Look for the toys at the bottom of the tub. Swish and slide your body back and forth in the water. Make waves. Oops, don't overflow!"

OVER AND UNDER

Chat while scrubbing, and draw attention to the following:

"Mark's hand is *on top of* the water. The washcloth is on the *bottom* of the tub. The soapsuds are floating *above* the water. Mark's feet are *under* the water."

or

"Can Mark splash his hands *in front of* his body? Now, can he splash *in back?* Push the soap *away.* Now bring it *near.* Put the soap *next to* the plastic boat. Now give the soap a sail *on* the boat."

COUNTING

Count each finger and toe as it is washed. Say, "Now we have washed one hand. How about washing two hands?" A child will sometimes beg to stay in the tub, in order to postpone bedtime. A good idea is to say, "Okay, you may take two swims up and two swims back, and then it's out you come."

Did you know, Susie, that momma salmon swim a long way upstream, when they are getting ready to lay their eggs? Every year they return to the same place to have their babies. How do you suppose they can remember where to go without a road map?

DRAMATIC PLAY

A child can pretend that a sponge is a boat; a container of spilled water is a waterfall; a washcloth wrapped around his hand is a puppet; the soap is a raft. Any floating toy makes good bathtime company.

WASHING HAIR

No guarantee to avoid tears and tantrums, for shampooing can often be frightening. A suggestion is the use of a hand-mirror. The child looks in it, while the adult soaps the hair. She watches (playing beauty parlor, perhaps) while her hair is smoothed down ("slicko"), or pushed up straight ("Indian"), or parted and plastered in the middle ("gigolo"). Hair gets clean as the style changes.

PHENOMENA

The tub is an ideal place to make simple observations of floating, displacement, wetness vs. dryness, temperature. Explanations are not necessary. This is the observation stage.

Try putting blown up balloons in the tub for the child who hates to take a bath. Inexpensive and expendable, they can be bounced around the tub to brighten the bathing.

Floating. Will the soap float? Some do not, so test to find out. Which toys float and which sink to the bottom? Do heavy things sink or float? Does the size make the difference or what it is made of? Why does the child not sink? Do some people float on water? How come?

Displacement. Place plastic containers in the tub. Fill with water. Now put a toy in the full container. Will the water overflow? Why, do you think?

Measurement. How many small boxes of water do we need to fill this large one? Can you pour the water from this container and make all of it fit in another one?

Temperature. Put your elbow in the top of the water, just before you get in the tub. Is the water too hot? Too cold? Just right?

Too Wet. All the fingers are wrinkled as a prune. All right, little one, time to come out of the tub.

Sometimes scientific "curiosity" leads to tasting. We remember a tot who thought the pretty soap looked good enough to eat, and did!

PLAY BATH

A "play bath" may do more good than punishment does. On trying days, an unhappy child can be dunked in a tepid tub to "cool off." The tub can also be a place to be when there is nothing to do and boredom is causing whining, fighting, or nagging.

Sit by the child while he plays with "tub toys" and take a minute to glance at that new magazine. It will be a cure for Mother as well! Tub toys can be the turkey baster, plastic bottles, sponges, plastic utensils, spatulas—(Look in the kitchen!). *Never leave a child alone in the tub.*

Dressing/ Undressing

The dawdler exists in every household. You are in a hurry, and Andy is staring into space, a sock dangling from his foot! You have firmly asked Linda to prepare for bed, and there she is, sitting on the floor, talking to her doll. Why should dressing be boring for children and such a source of aggravation for parents? By playing games, having fun, and creating a learning environment, you can turn a "sow's ear" into a "silk purse."

BODY PARTS

Sitter: If you will hurry up and take off your shirt, Jackie, we can play a game. It's an "I'm thinking of" game, the kind you love.

Jackie: Faster than the twinkling of an eye—swoosh—no shirt!

Sitter: Okay, what bends and has a point when you do, and doesn't when you don't?

Jackie: Sounds like a riddle. You forgot to say, "I'm thinking of." But I know anyway. My elbow!

Sitter: Smart boy. Okay, I'm thinking of something round and smooth with a tiny hole in the middle of it.

Jackie: My belly button?

Sitter: Now help me put your pajama top over your chest. Want to keep that heart inside nice and warm and loving.

Sing the song, "The jawbone connected to the neckbone, the neckbone connected to etc."

PLEASURE VS. PAIN

We all know the aspects of dressing that make it an ordeal. Perhaps you can discover what clothing gives discomfort, either in wearing or putting on and off. Children might move more quickly if it is explained what is going to happen when they are dressed, something, hopefully, they like to do!

Every morning a four-year-old boy whined and cried while his mother forced clothes upon his unwilling body. It was always the same battle of wills. The boy preferred certain jerseys and pants. The mother wanted to select that which fashionably "matched," something new, or something that Grandma had bought him. The child was too young to express himself. When he became older he knew how to explain that some shirts had seams that "itched," some pants had a snap that was too hard to open and close (when he went to the bathroom he had to fight it all the time), and turtle necks and heavy sweaters "squeezed" him. When he grew up, he wore only light and loose shirts. If only his mother had realized, what tears could have been spared.

Shoelaces.   These are a chief source of grief. Young children have poor coordination, which is why they are happy with fat crayons and big, soft balls. The same is true for laces. Thin nylon laces can be slippery, thick rope-type laces too bulky, and most laces are too short. Longer laces make shoe tying easier.

Shoe Chart.   Draw a large shoe on a piece of cardboard. Punch holes for lacing. Give the child a large, long shoelace for practice.

Shoe Bags.   Colorful shoebags on the backs of doors or closets make dressing more fun, and rooms more tidy. Not only may conventional footwear be stored in the bags, but also hats, mittens, socks, underwear, and a variety of small objects.

Shoes and Slippers.   Left or right, what child knows which is which? A child is helped by hints to remember left/right. A bracelet or toy watch may be worn on the *left* hand. The letter "L" may be painted on the sole of the appropriate shoe.

How tired the parents were of being disturbed in the morning! Every day they were awakened with the question, "Which slipper goes on which foot?" Then Mom had a brainstorm! She painted Todd's left big toenail with red polish. She also gave the left slipper the same dab. It was easy for him to match. The few extra winks each day was worth the effort.

Socks and Underwear.   Some children are more comfortable in cotton underwear that bodies can breathe in or socks that absorb the perspiration.

Zippers, Buttons, Hooks.   Some zippers work easily; some are always getting caught in the material or don't join together easily. Large fancy buttons or tiny buttons may be unmanageable. Hooks become bent; snaps stop working. Make certain the things your child wears are easy for him to get on and off. A friend had a lovely jacket that she seldom wore because it had tricky frogs which took "forever" to close.

COLORS

Try, while dressing and undressing, to use the name of the color of the article of clothing. Observe contrasting shades, if possible, i.e., the darker green rather than the very light green; the bright yellow, not the yellow that is dull; the tan sock; etc.

Vocabulary.   Basic colors are often mastered by the time a child enters first grade. However, why not sample the grand palette of colors that give us a wealth of "colorful" words: indigo, cerise, flamingo, chartreuse, ebony, etc.

COUNTING

A lagging dresser can be pepped up with appropriate rhymes: "One, two, buckle my shoe (do it!), three, four, shut the door (and that, too!)" How many fingers and toes? Are there the same number of toes on feet as fingers on hands? Play "One little, two little, three little Indians," holding up and putting down the child's fingers. Sing, "Ten little robins, sitting in a line, one flew away and then there were nine!" Teach, "Here is Thumbkin." If we hide our thumbs, how many fingers are left? What do we wear that has fingers on it? Why don't mittens? Why don't socks? (But have you seen the new toe socks?)

Play *Simon Says*, using the words "add" and "subtract":

Auntie: Simon Says add your shirt to your underwear. Simon Says add your pants. Simon Says add your socks. Subtract one sock. Oh, oh, I didn't say Simon Says.

Teenager: Simon Says subtract your blouse. Now Simon Says subtract your jumper. Simon Says put on your nightgown. Simon Says kiss me goodnight.

OVER AND UNDER

"Put your shoes *beside* the bed."

"Fold your sweater *inside* the drawer."

"Your yellow shirt buttons in the *back,* not like the green one that closes in *front.*"

"Put on your pajama *bottom,* and I'll help you with the pajama *top.*"

"Why do you suppose your panties are called *under*wear?"

"Climb *under* the blankets and let me tuck you *in*!"

Independence

A major thorn in parent–child survival is *unreasonable expectations.* The goal is the ultimate independence of the child. It helps for a five year old to be able to dress and undress in simple outer garments, including boots, by the time kindergarten begins. On the other hand, a two year old not only still needs assistance, but welcomes the comfort and conpanionship that go with it.

STEPS IN INDEPENDENCE

At first, the toddler receives total assistance. Then the child receives considerable assistance, but a few items are left to do alone. After helping put most of the clothes on, say, "Mommy is going now to put on her own dress. When I come back, will you be ready?"

Finally, the child is old enough to dress alone, but dawdles. Suggest a reward that will motivate his interest. "As soon as you are ready, I will have pancakes waiting." (The pleasure of parental attention is transferred to what happens after the task is completed.) A kitchen timer speeds action. Set it for 5 to 10 minutes. Explain that when the bell rings, it will be time to be ready. Watch the child race the clock.

With three preschoolers one mother could never decide when they were getting ready to go out whether to dress the children or herself first. If she dressed first, the gymnastics of preparing the children wrinkled and messed her good outfit. If she dressed them, they'd be dirty by the time she was ready! She solved the problem by putting on everything, except her outer clothing. She made up, donned jewelry, and topped her underwear with a robe. When the little ones were ready, it was merely a matter of minutes before she herself would be. This way, the odds were on her side!

DECISION MAKING

Encourage the choosing of one's own clothing, whenever possible. Preparing them the night before is reassuring. Shall it be the green corduroys with the yellow sweater, or the blue dungarees and the orange-and-red-striped jersey?

DRESSING THE TEDDY

Some children want their toys to enjoy every experience they do. This can include dress-and-bedtime.

Mom: I'll help you undress for bed. Then you put Teddy's p.j.'s on him too. (Have you saved outgrown clothing for the toys to wear?)

Dad: My, what a fast bedtime-get-readier you are! And what's this? All the dolls dressed and ready for bed, too?

MEASUREMENTS

A *height* chart should be a standard bedroom decoration. Periodically, mark off how big we are growing. When comparing the heights of members of the family, why not include willing pets, and even toys?

Weight is often watched by the adults in the family. The undressed child will enjoy climbing on the *bathroom scale*. What differences there are in scales! Is the one at home like the one in the bus station, like Aunt Ida's baby scale, like the doctor's, like the one in the grocery or delicatessen?

EXERCISES

Parent and child, stripped to underpants, or nude, can take time for quick stretches and bends. Can we reach the ceiling? Touch our toes? Bend five times from the waist?

Love-Ins HOW MUCH?

"Do I love you this much?" (Hold out arms close together.)   "No".

"This much?" (Arms further apart.)   "No".

"This much?" (Arms wide; child runs into them.)   "Yes!"

KISSES

• *Sugar bowl kisses*—Gently hold each others' ears as you kiss.

• *Eskimo kisses*—Rub noses.

• *Fish face kisses*—Pucker lips and kiss without laughing.

- *Winky blinkies*—Open and close eye gently on cheek, so that cheek is brushed with eyelashes.

- *Frog face kisses*—Carefully pinch cheeks of each other. Mouth draws out into a frog face. Kiss if you can!

VISITORS

- *Ring bell*—Pull gently on hair.

- *Knock at doors*—Knock on forehead.

- *Lift latch*—Gently lift eyelid.

- *Peek in*—Gently lift nose.

- *Walk in*—Put fingers quickly into and out of mouth.

- *Go way down cellar and eat apples*—Tickle neck as if walking downstairs to Adam's apple at neck!

FALLING KISSES

Child pretends kisses are falling from his body; adult tries to catch them. Child touches his arm and says, "Here's one." Adult catches kiss by kissing the spot on the arm. Child touches leg; adult catches kiss before it "falls off" the leg.

MAGIC CIRCLE

Adult makes believe he draws a large circle on the child's stomach and says, "Draw a magic circle and end it with a dot." Adult then dots middle of circle on child's tummy. Magic circles can be drawn on backs, arms, heads, etc. Child squirms to avoid getting the tickling dot.

MAKE UP A  RITUAL FOR YOUR CHILDREN.

WAITING PLACES

Whether traveling or merely visiting the local doctor, waiting times can be the most difficult times of all for children. How hard it is for them to be still when natural instincts are to wiggle and giggle. The following games are as suitable for railroad and airport lounges as they are for offices of any kind that keep people waiting. It is always a good idea to keep some small, interesting objects with you. Pipe cleaners; colored, assorted elastic bands; a cloth book; a pencil; and a small pad of paper are some suggestions for these trying moments.

Counting   What a fascinating variety and number of objects found in public places! What fun it is to count them. How many people? How many are men, women, and children? Can the child count all the red items? Can we help him count the signs, the magazines, the jackets on the hooks? If it is a place with few items to look at (such as at an outdoor bus station), why not count the objects in your purse or pockets!

Sharp Eyes

Uncle Roger: Would you be a good detective if you had to be? Can you sharpen up your eyes and remember what you see?

Stevie: Sure, just try me!

Uncle Roger: Well, suppose you take a good, long look at this room. Then close your eyes and tell me everything you can remember. Wait, I have an idea. I'll keep score. Ten things will buy you an ice cream.

Magazines   A child does not need to read to enjoy looking at a book. In addition to reading aloud to him, play games with the words themselves.

Letters.   Show the child a specific letter, e.g., "s." Ask the child to find every "s" on the page. At first the finger will point helter skelter. Left-right and top-to-bottom is good preparation for reading. An older child may be able to circle the particular letter with a pencil. Begin with distinctively different letters (first s, then, perhaps, m), rather than letters that are tricky for children, such as p and q or b and d).

Pictures.   Suggest that the child find specific objects in pictures. "Can you find a big tree? Show me a picture with a mother in it. Is there one with a black car, or a truck?"

Don't overlook the potential for vocabulary developing in this situation. Use colorful, descriptive adjectives whenever possible. Instead of "truck," you might say "dump truck," "Mack truck," "pick-up truck." Keep *expanding* concepts.

Pretend Stories.   Look carefully at pictures together and talk about them. Who are the people? What are they doing? What might happen next? Imaginations stretch by pretending what happened before the pictured experience.

Adult:	Here is a picture of a family at a picnic. Can you tell me what they are doing?
Child:	Hmmm, the mother is putting out the food. The dad is lifting a picnic basket. The kids are running.
Adult:	Where do you suppose they are going to eat? Is the mother putting the food on the ground?
Child:	No, it is too cold.
Adult:	How can you tell?
Child:	Well, they are wearing warm jackets. Besides, you can tell it isn't summer by the trees. [This would be a fabulous observation for a child to make.]
Adult:	Well then, where do you think they plan to have that picnic? Do you see any picnic tables?
Child:	Maybe the edge of the back of the station wagon?
Adult:	Yes, that is called tailgaiting, and people sometimes do that at a football game. What do you think this family will do after the picnic?
Child:	Why, go to the game, I guess!

Remembering. The child looks at the picture, closes the book, and tries to remember what was in the picture. This is a good game for adults to do, also. Try keeping score by giving a point for each remembered object. Take into consideration age and skill differences, and give older players a point handicap.

Textures

Public places are often better for touching than residences. We do not encourage running hands along your living room walls, but the walls of a railroad or bus waiting room often have interesting textures. Are they rough or smooth? Are they wood, concrete, stucco, stone, brick, painted plaster? Are they cold or warm to the touch?

Vocabulary. Teach children the names of materials. An inquisitive child may ask where the material comes from. Does it grow in the ground or is it made in a factory? Games can be played around this concept. Where did they get that stone wall? Do you know where the wood for these paneled walls comes from? When children talk about how something "feels" or "tastes" or "smells," their vocabulary reveals the poetry of the unencumbered mind.

We knew a little girl whose vocabulary was tinted by the "feel" of things: "Chillerator," "underbrella," and "spits" (for orange pits).

Metals and Fabrics

Large public waiting rooms are treasure troves for "people-watching," as well as providing innumerable materials and articles to talk about and compare.

Clothing. Discuss colors, fabrics, weight, texture of either the family itself or that of any other person in the waiting room. Needless to say, this is not intended to be within earshot of the people being discussed.

Furnishings. The furnishings of places that are not found in a home fascinate young people. Talk about the magazine stand, vending machines, or refreshment booths. Examples are:

• The gum and candy machines. (Who fills them? How and when?)

• The bubbling punch machine dispensing both orange and purple liquid pick-ups in many stations.

- The lady who sells the magazines and newspapers. (Where does she come from, do you suppose, and does anyone help her? Does she get lonely? Does she like what she does? Why?)

- Blower-type hand dryers in many restrooms are nothing like the towels at home. (What fun to use! What makes them work?)

- Put a penny or a nickel in the big scale sometimes found in stations. That needle swinging up does not resemble one in any scale in a house.

Clinics

While waiting in a hospital or clinic, draw attention to "what is different" from that which is found in a home. The *medical scale* is different from a baby scale, a grocery scale, or the kind parents climb on to groan on. *Charts* and *posters* offer stimulating topics for conversation. The *rolling bed* and *wheel chair* intrigue youngsters. The attire on the staff, blood pressure gauges, light reflectors, stethoscopes, etc. are resources for discussion. "Why, why?" is the common refrain. Preschoolers want to know! Understanding alleviates anxiety.

Some clinics have long benches. If there is room to do so, let a little one stretch out on his back and study the ceiling. Tiles and light fixtures may be commonplace to an adult, but if they are different from a little one's own environment, they provide a design for his imagination. Looking at the world from a horizontal position is highly suitable to the very young.

Isometrics

Long waits cramp bodies of all ages. The child will want to stretch, and you may need to as well. Where this is not feasible (i.e., a crowded doctor's office), exercise in one place.

Deep Breaths.   Begin by alternating deep and shallow breaths; the adult begins, and the child follows. Then count to five while holding a deep breath and let it out slowly. Now take three or more breaths together. Play a breathing game. Let one player adopt a breathing pattern (two longs, one short, for instance) and the other mimic.

Hands.   Push palms of hands together and count to five; relax; count to five; press and relax several times.

Feet. Press your feet to the floor. (A child will have to be sitting on a chair or bench low enough for him to reach the floor easily with his feet.) Lift the heels slightly, in a relaxed position. Alternate pressing and lifting. Count to five for each position. His little legs will feel better already.

Letter Sounds

Pick a simple letter sound such as "b." What can the players see that begins with that sound?

Gramps: I am thinking of a ball and bat. That boy must be going to a Little League game. Can you think of a word that begins like ball?

Carol: Boy!

Gramps: Good. What else?

Carol: There is a lady in the snack shop eating a bagel. Oh, Grandpa, can I have one too?

Now change the letter sound to "M." Play another game using the "S" sound.

Following Directions

The adult gives the child two or three simple directions to follow. Can he remember them? Perhaps he is given ten points for every action he follows correctly. In confined places, make the directions something he can do while sitting (i.e., clap three times, stamp your foot twice). In large places, let the activity be an excuse to let the child have a limited roaming experience. For example, have him walk to the door, turn around, and come back; or walk to the bench, sit on it, return; or walk to the candy counter, buy a snack bar, bring it back to Dad.

When we taught first grade, a device for a wriggling pupil was to send him with a note to a distant teacher. The note merely read, "Send him back."

Verbalizing

Stories. Repeating familiar fairy stories is the best standby of all. Pass the time by beginning a story and letting the child finish. Initiate original stories and let the child pick up the story line. (This is very difficult, and the adult should be content with very simple tales.)

Rhyming.   Adult says a word and the child comes up with a word that sounds alike.

- spot/pot
- cat/bat
- cake/rake

Not enough emphasis can be placed on giving children this auditory training needed for reading. And don't forget the Mother Goose rhymes.

I'm Thinking Of.

Aunt Polly:	I'm thinking of someone who comes to your house on Christmas Eve.
Randy:	Santa!
Aunt Polly:	I'm thinking of something round, red, sweet, on a stick.
Randy:	A lollipop!
Aunt Polly:	Yes, and here you are!

Count Up.   Someone begins a counting game, to develop understanding of sequence. Keep it in the low numbers if that is the extent of the child's ability.

Adult:	I'm thinking of one dog.
Child:	I'm thinking of two cats.
Child:	I'm thinking of three bears.
Adult:	I'm thinking of four chickens.

Puppets   Use any object for a puppet: pencil, crayon, nail file, rolled-up paper, mitten, glove, hankies, tissues, fingers. The adult begins the action game by saying, "Hello, what are you doing here?" The child quickly catches on and responds with whatever he devises for his "puppet." The play can be centered on the reasons they are in the waiting place. If the child is experiencing any anxiety about what he is waiting for (the trip, the doctor), this is a good way to work it out. Those with a highly developed sense of humor can make up nonsense plays.

What, an hour has passed, and we're still waiting? Any doctor who keeps a child waiting that long deserves the consequences. Okay, little one, lie or crawl on the floor. We've tried to keep you busy. Now you're on your own!

EATING OUT

The joy of eating out is often diminished by the restlessness of young children. While waiting for service, here are some techniques to survive.

I Spy

Dad: I see someone wearing an apron. Who is it?

Polly: The waitress!

Mom: I see something pointy on the bottom, round on the top.

Junior: Is it a person or a thing?

Polly: Is it big or little?

Mom: It is something you can carry. It is good to eat.

Polly and Junior: An ice cream cone!

Whispers

Whisper a simple sentence to a child. He whispers it to the next person. That person repeats the whisper to another, and so on. The last person says the sentence aloud. Is it the same as the first one? Rarely!

Colors

Begin a game by saying "I am thinking of something green. Is it in the salad? Is it the lettuce? Is it the dress on the lady in the next booth? Is it the plant at the window?" Use as many colors as it takes for the food to come.

Objects

"I am thinking of something round. It has legs. It is brown. Yes, it is the table."
"I am thinking of something shiny. No, it is not the napkin holder. No, it is not the silverware. Yes, it is the grill the cook is making our hamburgers on."

Table Games *Toothpicks.* Make piles from the toothpicks. Ask the child to make a pile of three toothpicks. Can he make four? Can he make designs? Lay them out into a house shape. Pretend you have a family living in it. Assorted coins can represent the figures. Dimes for little ones, perhaps, and quarters for the adults.

Salt and Pepper Shakers. Teach prepositions, in front of, before, behind, on top of, etc.

Mother: Can you put the salt shaker in front of the sugar bowl? Can you put it on top of the napkin? Can you put the napkin under the pepper shaker?

Spoons and Forks. Arrange and rearrange the silverware into patterns. Lay three spoons and two forks in a row. Can the child copy what he sees? For more abstract skills, repeating the "pattern" can be an exercise: two forks, one knife, two forks, and . . . ?

Napkins. Fold the napkins into triangles, squares, and rectangles. The adult does it; the child copies; or the adult merely folds the napkin into a shape and asks the little one if it is a square or a triangle. A napkin can cover a dish. Is it on top of it? Is it under it? Think of all the things you can do with a napkin!

What's Missing? The child studies the place settings on the table. While his or her eyes are closed, an object is removed. Perhaps it is a spoon or fork. The child must tell what was taken away.

Categories What goes together? Cups-and-saucers. Salt-and-pepper shakers. Forks-and-spoons.

- What categories do these objects fall into?
- Forks and spoons—silverware
- Oranges and apples—fruit
- Peas and carrots—vegetables

- Tomatoes, lettuce, onions, peppers—salad

- Pie, ice cream, brownies—dessert

Dramatic Play

Fold a napkin so that it resembles a bow tie. Dramatize the old melodrama "pay the rent." The villain twists his napkin over his lip to resemble a mustache. The girl pretends it is a bow atop her head. The hero wears it as a bow tie.

Villain: Pay the rent.

Girl: I can't pay the rent.

Villain: Pay the rent.

Girl: I won't pay the rent.

Hero: I'll pay the rent.

Villain: Curses. Foiled again!

What else can a napkin represent for dramatic play? Can it be a blindfold, a flag of truce, a handkerchief, a bandage? Using a napkin for the "kick-off," see how far imagination will leap. Don't be surprised, however, if the only thing it suggests is food. In a restaurant, it may be hard to think of anything else.

Drape a knife or fork with a napkin, and create a puppet. Two or more players may engage in a puppet show while waiting to be served.

Mind Stretching

Play guessing games about that which cannot be seen, but must be imagined.

- What happens in the kitchen?

- What items are used to make our dinner?

- Where do hamburgers come from? Lobsters? Ice cream?

- Where do you suppose the people at the next table are going to from here? Where do you think they come from?

- What kind of jobs do people have who work in the restaurant? How many jobs can you name?

Faces "Can you make a sad face? A happy face? An angry face? A hungry face?"

Tell Along Begin a story and let the next person continue it. It can be a familiar story or a nonsense one, or it can be a highly imaginative one. For example, "Once upon a time Mr. Salt and Mrs. Pepper met in a Howard Johnson ..." (Can you continue?)

Hot and Cold What is hot? Soup, tea, coffee? What is cold? Cokes, ice cream, Jello?

People Places How many boys can you count? Are there more tall people than short ones? How many are eating? How many are talking? How many are waiting *patiently* like we are? How many are playing games to help pass the time?

FIELDS AND FORESTS

The outdoors presents a vast wonderland of discoveries. Open spaces is a key word today. It is also a way of describing the attitude families often have when enjoying the outdoors. Be open and flexible. The world is full of surprises. The unexpected colors any experience. With little ones, the unexpected is the expected anyway!

Sometimes your outdoors will be a stroll to a neighborhood park or playground. Playgrounds come with built-in recreation; take the time to talk to other mothers or fathers, and think of the playground as your playtime. Sometimes the park will be a reservation, a state park, a forest, or the woods around a lake. Even families with very young children take to the outdoors by camping or trailer living. All of the outside becomes a vast playground!

Cloud Gazing
Lie back and imagine pictures in the clouds: Two cotton balls bumping? A tree? A herd of sheep? Two white horses charging across the plain? The constant changes make this an endlessly absorbing activity.

Body Squiggles
Open spaces lend themselves to stretching the muscles. Plenty of room to walk on your hands like a crab, hop like a jumping bean, gallop like a horse. How easy it is for a field of grass to become a stage for silly actions.

Obstacle Course
Can the little one walk around a large tree, crawl under the park bench, and touch the little evergreen at the edge of the grass? Simple directions with no more than two or three obstacles should do. In the playground, the directions could be to walk around the sandbox, climb on and off a swing, and hop to the refreshment stand!

Colors

Mom:	I spy something blue and white.
Dad:	The sky and clouds.
Mom:	I spy something red, orange, yellow, and green.
Tommy:	Oh, I give up.
Mom:	The maple tree.
Dad:	I spy something grayish.
Robin:	Is it the old dead log?
Mom:	I'm thinking of something green to walk on.
Rusty:	Grass! Now let me think of one. I know! I'm thinking of something black, and white a little.
Mom:	Hmmm, the newspaper?
Rusty:	No.
Mom:	My shoes?
Rusty:	One more guess, and you lose.
Mom:	The tires on the car over there?
Rusty:	No. That dog with spots!

Balancing

No child can resist walking along a wall, a railroad tie, or a curb. Placing one foot in front of the other, and holding an adult's hand, is a feat of balance. It is a precarious accomplishment. A wall can make for a history lesson.

A long time ago farmers found many rocks and stones in their fields. They could not plant their crops with so many stones in the ground. As they worked very hard to lift them, they piled them on top of one another, at the edges of their property, until they had surrounded the land they owned with walls of rocks. That way, each farmer could tell where his farm ended and his neighbor's began. Walls are fun to hide behind, too. Do you know how they were used in this fashion long ago? In Massachusetts, the farmers turned themselves into soldiers, to fight the British. At that time this country belonged to the King of England. The farmers took their long guns (muskets) and became soldiers "in a minute." That is why the first army our country had was called "The Minute Men."

Walking the Plank.   Pirate tales often include "walking the plank." Few children would understand what a "plank" is, but once understood, it is fun to pretend to be pirates. Use a picnic bench, a park bench, a smooth wall, or a fallen log. Very young children may begin by "walking the path," and progress to higher "planks," as ability and confidence grow.

Over and Under

Dad: Here is our collection of nature's treasures. Can we play a game with them? Bobby, can you put two acorns *in* mother's purse? Say, how about making a row of shiny pebbles *under* the bench? Can you place one cat-tail *on* each of our sweaters?

Amy: Let's play hide and find! I'll put my twigs *under* things. See if you can tell where I hide them. Now guess!

Larry: Are they *under* the bench? Are they *under* the picnic basket? Or maybe the blanket?

People Places

Wherever there are people, play memory games, and sharpen skills of observation. The child takes a long look, then he closes his eyes and he must tell what he remembers. "Hmm, let me think. A man sleeping. A lady knitting. A dog. A baby in a carriage."

As vocabulary matures, encourage children to use sentences and details of colors, sizes, shapes, and activities.

"The man is sleeping with his shirt off. He is snoring. A fat lady is scolding her child. The child is muddy. The baby in the carriage is sucking his fingers."

Creative Dramatics

"Let's pretend" is as natural to children as breathing. It is easily played in roles. "Can you pretend to be another person?" "An animal?" "How about something not alive at all?"

And when Jack climbed down the beanstalk, he chopped it down. The giant came crashing upon the ground with the beanstalk. . . . How do you think the *beanstalk* felt? Did it mind being climbed? Did it feel better when Jack climbed it than when the giant did? How did it feel when the giant crashed with it? Can you show me? What do you suppose happened after that? Did the beanstalk grow up again?

PRETEND-TO-BE GAMES

- A piece of grass.

- Two trees blowing in the wind.

- One cloud bumping into another.

- A dead log that is a home for rabbits.

- A family of tall marsh grass.

- A cluster of pine cones or berries on a branch.

- Two evergreens standing guard before a door.

- The bark that protects a large old tree.

- The nest no longer used by the gone-away robins.

- Two large rocks jutting from a cliff.

- The park bench.

- The sand in the sandbox.

OFFSHOOTS OF PRETEND-TO-BE GAMES

At home the child may recall his feelings and emotions by dictating a "story" about the object he pretended to be. Or he may have become very interested in that abandoned nest and want to "write" about it or illustrate it. Creative dramatics is the beginning of empathy.

What you did when you were a cloud was beautiful. You made me feel you really were a cloud. It was like watching a story. Would you like me to write it down for you and read it back? Or would you like to draw a picture of how you think the cloud feels? We can put the story and picture together, and why, do you know what, it will be like a book.

Trail Blazers Prescouting tracking activities can set the stage for future woodsmen or women. Mark some trees in the woods with colored chalk. Call the children to look for the special trees. They follow them along, until they come to a treasure, or "secret place." At the end of the trail, place a basket of cookies. Make it simple enough, so that the children will find the cookies before other hungry forest visitors do.

Tramp through a field of high grass. Let your footsteps mat the grass sufficiently so that children can follow your path.

Older children would love to mark the trail, pretending to be Indian guides. Lay a trail of sticks on a pineneedle floor in the woods. Can the younger warriors tiptoe through the forest, as nimble-footed as Indian braves?

"Children, you remember the story of Hansel and Gretel, don't you? That was a very scary story that had a happily-ever-after ending. When the children were lost in the woods, what smart thing did they do to keep from getting lost? Dropping the bread crumbs was the same as marking a trail. Alas, the birds ate up all the clues, and if they had not, Hansel and Gretel would never have met the wicked old witch!"

Conversation

Why is the grass green? Why are some trees taller than others? Why do leaves turn colors? Why do some trees stay green all year? Why does it rain? Is the sun hot? Where does it go at night? Where do the stars come from?

Camouflage

A simple explanation of how Mother Nature protects her animals begins with matching colors.

Dad: Look, Jerry, if I lay mom's green scarf on the grass, do you think you could see it from a distance? Now, son, suppose I tuck your brown shoes on that tree branch?

Play camouflaging games with first one member of a group and then another hiding objects in places where it would be difficult to distinguish the colors. Next, ask children to try to think of which animals hide themselves this way.

• The brown weasel in summer becomes the white ermine in winter.

• Chameleons are very clever. They change color to suit the background.

• Polar bears are white against the snow.

• In the Florida Everglades, you have to look very closely to tell if the alligator is a log, or perhaps made of mud.

In the army, soldiers sometimes wear uniforms colored with green all over the brown. If the soldier is going to fight in the jungle, or crawl through the woods, he would not like the enemy to see him from the distance. From the air, the soldier would look like part of the forest. This protection, called "army camouflage," was a lesson learned from our animal friends.

Safety Rules.   This topic leads easily to another important one. When walking in the dark, a person blends with the darkness, unless he or she wears something bright. This is one time when we do not want to be camouflaged!

Rhyme Time   Pass the time with rhyming games:

- The fly in the sky

- The ant on the plant

- The worm that can squirm

- The stone all alone

What else can you think of?

Telling the Time   *Shadows.*   Shadows are fun to chase and step on. They also indicate time. We leave large shadows as the day grows short. The high noon sun gives us a tiny shadow. Draw a child's attention to the difference and relate them to the passing of time.

Nature Sounds.   Sharp ears will recognize country sounds that are clues to the time of day. Frogs croak at night, as do certain crickets. Do we hear an owl in the distance? Some birds greet the morning cheerily, while others signal the coming of evening.

Smells   Lie in the grass and smell it. Does lawn grass smell differently than field grass? Scoop handfuls of pine needles. How do they smell? Explain that pine is often used to scent soap and men's shaving lotions. Grandmothers sewed them into pillows to create nice-smelling rooms. In examining the phenomena of the park, encourage touching but don't overlook the pathways to learning that smelling opens up. If a child can tell you "how it smells," you may hear language used in a colorful and original way.

Comparison Games   Observe differences in familiar objects:

Sis: What is the biggest thing you can see?

Judy: That big old tree.

Sis: Okay, now what is the smallest?

Judy: A teensy-weensy pebble.

Sis: What is bigger, the pine cone or the acorn?

Judy: I'll show you the biggest cone, and then I'll find the
smallest one.

Touch and Feel

See and touch a variety of objects found outdoors. What differences are there in sizes and types: Does the tuft of pine needles have three or five needles? Is a chestnut larger than an acorn? How soft is the moss around the trees? Cat-tails, marsh grasses, milkweed pods, berry clusters, cones and seeds lend themselves to touch and comparison. Each region suggests its own natural wonders such as cacti in the Southwest and wheat shafts in the Midwest.

Pine Needles.   Pines give us a variety of needles. Stroking the tufts across a hand is soothing. Make a pile and bury your nose in it to awaken the senses. Do they feel prickly? How many needles on a sprig? Some have more than others, some are stubby, others graceful. In a single forest, are there many kinds of pine trees? Some look almost blue (the blue spruce). Do you see differences in the shades of green? *Vocabulary:* Describing nature is the beginning of poetry. Prickly, stubby, needles, tufts are words used in a context new to a child.

Acorns.   Who would believe that "large oaks from little acorns grow"? Use the little acorn cap for assorted dishes. Sort them according to size and shapes. Can we have an acorn family?

Leaves.   Are all leaves alike? Examine the leaves common to your area: a majestic palm leaf, a small elm leaf, a "fingery" oak leaf. But watch out for the cactus leaf. It does not want to be touched!

Stones.   Stones can be smooth or rough, large or small, colored or white, valuable or common. They can line a garden, decorate a window, become imaginary people, be made into jewelry, or just be enjoyed as collections.

Touch

Place all the collected treasures in a large bag. Have the child feel inside and try to identify the object by touching. As he takes each one out, he calls out, "a pine cone, an acorn, a feather," etc.

Feathers.   A poet wrote, "When a bird drops a feather, it is a present, meant just for you...." Collect feathers, feel their softness, and observe their size, shape, and colors. They make soft piles in a shoebox; they make designs pasted to cardboard; they can become birds when drawn around on a sheet of paper to which they have been glued. What's more, an interest in feathers can lead to curiosity about the birds that sent them on their way to us. It is a wonderful experience to walk in a field, spy objects on forest floors, look out for birdfeeders, and become alert to spring and fall migrations. Regard a found feather as a personal treasure.

Clover.   Direct your attention to grass. Is grass all the same? Why, here is something different: a clover. Clover has three leaves. What luck to find a four-leaf clover.

... Lucky clover ... Long ago in far-off Ireland, the folks believed the lucky elves, called leprechauns, would come to their homes if a good luck charm was left for them. The four-leaf clover, they discovered, would bring the little men to their doors. Of course, this is a fairy tale, believed by the children of Ireland, but to this day, everywhere you go in the world, people look for a four-leaf clover to bring them good fortune.

Cones.   The outdoors is for touching. Pine cones are rough, multishaped, and sized, and fun to sort. They can be lined up into "families." What roles do your little ones assign to them? Tall ones for father, round ones for mother?

Sharp Ears   *Noise* is identifiable. Specific noises take place in cities and zoos and parks and railroad stations. In the park, close your eyes and listen for the sounds.

Nancy: I hear boys playing ball. One shouts, "Safe!"

Todd: I hear someone calling, "Higher, higher." Must be pushing a swing.

Chuckie: I hear a funny chirping. No, it doesn't sound like a bird. Hey, everyone, open your eyes. There is a squirrel eating our picnic!

What sounds can you make with nature's treasures? Take a stick and tap a tree; then tap another kind of tree. Do they sound the same? Rub stones together; hit them together; toss them into a sandpile, at a tree, or in a bucket. Large stones make different sounds than small ones.

Do acorns or pine cones rubbed together, or one against the other (that is, a pine cone against an acorn) make specific sounds? Do acorns sound "crunchy"? Hitting trees with a stone, an acorn, a pine cone, a shell, creates sound. Does a stone wall send off the same sounds when hit with different objects?

Vocabulary.   It is fascinating to discover the words a young child uses to describe what he hears: scrunchy, roughish, hardish, coldish. There will be no wrong or right words, only poetry!

Stillness is a quality in itself to be appreciated and observed.

The sun is fading, and we are stretched on our backs, eyes drooping. It is the end of a long, restful day. Soon we will gather our gear and head back to the real world. One last moment to savor the solitude. What sounds does even the stillness offer? Do you hear an owl hooting in the distance? Does a chickadee signal her mate, "come home, come home!" Are there distant shouts, perhaps, of others leaving the park for the day? Can we hear the sun go down? The flowers close? The stars come out? An imaginative child will pretend to hear even silence. What does it say?

Sally: Listen everyone, I can hear the sun dropping into the ground!

Don't forget the old standbys:

- Leap frog

- Tag

- Hide and seek

- Red light

- Giant steps

- Kick the can

- Sardines

Collections   NATURE'S TREASURES

- Acorns

- Chestnuts

- Dried grasses, berries
- Cat-tails
- Milkweed pods
- Rocks, pebbles
- Shells
- Pine cones
- Sunflower seeds
- Colored leaves
- Pine tufts
- Feathers
- Corn stalks

USES FOR COLLECTIONS

Shoe Boxes. Shoe boxes seem to be just the right size for a collection of stones, acorns, shells, whatever. It can be great fun on the "what'll I do?" rainy day to line up the shiny pebbles so that they make imaginary soldiers; or let the pine cones become pretend families with personalities based on shapes and sizes. And when the play time is over, the boxes stack and store easily.

Crafts.

1. Glue acorns, pine cones, seeds, and dried berries to a board in a design. Shellac the plaque. This makes a delightful wall decoration or door hanging.

2. Use small pebbles to glue to a board in the form of a mosaic; or combine pebbles, seeds, and other small objects to create a mixed media collage.

3. Paint cones and glue into a wreath.

4. Cut a hole in an acorn, put a straw in it, and make a pipe.

5. Make a hole in the bottom of a pine cone, put a stick in it, and create a stick puppet.

6. Pine needles sewed between two sections of cloth make a heavenly smelling pillow.

7. Colored leaves pressed between two pieces of waxed paper make charming fall placemats.

8. Corn husks make up into a doll.

9. Use nature to depict nature: grass pasted to paper for grass, cat-tails for trees, shells for clouds.

Store.   Visit crafts fairs and see how many familiar objects have been turned into ornaments. Painted rock paperweights are standard items. Wild flowers artfully arranged make beautiful year round bouquets. Creative children might enjoy selling their products for a nominal sum of money. The proceeds could go to a favorite charity.

Gifts.   Children seldom have the opportunity to give a gift they have made themselves. A hand-created art object can have more meaning than a commercial one.

Museums.   Use carton boxes, benches, picnic tables, or card tables for display counters. Lay out the treasures according to categories. (Categorizing is a vital learning skill!) With the help of an older child or adult, the objects can be labeled. The museum may be a "natural history" one, or be specialized. If rocks, for example, are being shown, invite neighbors and friends to a "geology exhibit."

KITCHEN CLASSROOM

The kitchen can be a vast playschool if you give it that perspective. Try to see it from a small person's view. It has such a variety of objects, colors, shapes, sizes, and textures! Never permit the child, however, to play with sharp objects, knives, electric appliances, electrical cords, hot water, or pots on a stove. Supervision in the kitchen is always a good idea, especially when cooking is taking place.

Touch Place several familiar objects in a paper bag, and have the child close his or her eyes and feel inside the bag. Can a spoon be identified? Why does it feel different from the fork? Comparing the texture, weight or temperature of familiar objects is a lesson in simple science.

- Paper towels/terry towels

- Plastic bowls/metal bowls

- Apples/oranges

- Raw vegetables/cooked vegetables

- Dry cereal/cooked cereal (feeling here should be done with the tongue!)

Smell Kitchens can awaken all sensory perceptions. They are synonymous with sniffing.

Do homebaked breads, waffles, and cakes smell the same as berries, strawberry jam, or Jello? Why does sniffing an onion make you cry? Does a garlic bud smell like a rose bud?

Reading Readiness

SHAPES

For a child to distinguish letters he or she has to distinguish shapes first. The ability to read is based on developing fine perception in the preschool years. The gross differences between squares, circles, and triangles will easily be transferred to the acute differences between p, b, q, and d. These letters may look to children like balloons on a stick. Others confuse color, order, or sound.

Mom: Can you tell me how many things you see in the kitchen that are round?

Bobby: Clock, pan, pie plate, dish, light, you!

Dad: While we're getting dinner, son, let's play a game. I'll be thinking of something square and see if you can guess.

Robin: Mmm, is it the cake pan? Is it the table? Is it the oven? Oh, is it the cake?

LEFT-TO-RIGHT

Another important facet of reading is left-to-right eye movement. While most very young children can't yet identify their left and right hand, they should be aware that each side of the body has this identification.

Table-setting is a simple task that teaches coordination, left and right, and math. There must be a spoon for each place setting, a knife, etc. Have the child place all the knives around the table, then all the forks, then the spoons, and so on rather than one place setting at a time; it is too hard for him to remember the order of silverware. Remind him that some things go on the *left*, others the *right*. Draw a pattern at which the child can glance as he moves around the table.

COLORS

All the primary colors can be found in a kitchen. Never ask for or identify any object without calling its color.

Sally: Please hand me that red potholder. Now may I please have that orange sponge? I'll be needing salad greens for dinner. Can you get them from the fridge?

SIZES AND AMOUNTS

Make every opportunity to compare sizes as you cook. Point out the large pan versus the small one. Ask for a tall glass as opposed to a short one. Ask if the child wants the dish with the most raisins or the least. Ask if he thinks there is more milk in one glass or another.

TEXTURES

He can also compare textures felt on the hand and on the tongue:

- bumpy potatoes

- scratchy onions

- pebbly crackers

- rough carrots

- silky pudding

- oily dressing

- stringy cheese

- tangy mustard

- crackly nuts

- crunchy celery

- tickly soft drinks

- icicly popsicles

- sippy (through a straw) milkshakes

- soothing sherbert

- chunky peanut butter

- sticky honey

- chewy caramel

SOUNDS

Auditory discrimination is what teachers call listening for the differences in the sounds of words. Another way to say this is phonics and much of the approach to teaching reading is based on this technique. As in perceiving visual differences, a child must also perceive auditory differences. Begin with simple kitchen sounds.

Mom: Close your eyes and tell me what you hear.

Chip: The electric mixer.

Mom: Now what?

Chip: Water running.

Mom: What does this sound like?

Chip: I give up. Oh nuts in the chopper. Can I chop them?

Beat a pan softly with a spoon, tap an empty oatmeal box (makes a good homemade drum or maraca filled with dried beans), bang a pan cover against the pan, strike a knife against a glass half-filled with water, and if you have real crystal snap your fingernail against it and hear it sing.

VOCABULARY

Cooking has a language of its own: sauce, gel, grease, dice, scrape, peel, beat, ice (frost), whip, set, preserve, can. When used as *verbs* these words have new meaning to a child!

A wonderful book, "A Bear Before Breakfast" pinpoints this vocabulary problem. The parents say "He eats like a horse" and the child imagines someone with a feedbag on; they speak of selling a "white elephant" down the street, and the child runs to the door to see this fabulous creature. Kitchen vocabulary is a brand new language to a child.

Some of the many wonderous words and terms to be found here are rind, shortening, stew, blend, fold in, foamy, frothy, bubbly, steaming, rack, beaters, chilled, dressing, stuffing, mold, pickled, sweet-and-sour, vinegar, mayo, BLT, à la mode, lyonnaise, au gratin, broiled, roasted, pan-fried, hash-browned, toasted, browned, simmer, sautée, slivered, shredded, spatula.

Some of the wonderous things to be found here are blenders, micro-ovens, mini-toasters, strainers, graters, sieves, electric knives, cocktail shakers, ice tongs, ice crushers, collanders, coffee makers, coffee grinders, hot trays, chafing dishes, fondu pots, oven timers, preset ovens, roasting pans, pressurized squirt cans (for whip cream), nut choppers, dinner bells, candles of any kind.

Categories   The kitchen is where to begin to learn categories: fruit, vegetables, meat, baked goods, bread and rolls, fresh, canned, frozen, cooked, spices, baking supplies, treats, beverages, cheeses, and cereals.

Since most people organize their shelves and cabinets along these lines, a child may learn to store food after a shopping trip or replace something after it has been used.

Grandma: Sweetie, if you can get down the baking powder in the red and white can, the jar of honey and the big flour canister, I think we'll bake some bread.

An imaginative mother used Madison Avenue techniques to whet her toddler's appetite. Exotic words described ordinary food. Thus cottage cheese surrounded with pineapple chunks was a "sunshine salad," and she took liberties with a Western sandwich to call the egg filling "a souffle." One day a sitter was close to tears trying to please her gourmet charge, who was ordering a "souffle" like mommy makes.

Reading

Many children learn to read some words before entering school by identifying the labels on food. Much of this is reinforced on television. Begin with soup cans and have the child match those with the same letters: PEA TOMATO CHICKEN (the latter is easiest because it usually has a chick on the can). Breakfast cereals can almost always be read, because there is so much bombardment of these words on television. Sorting the cans according to label is an excellent preschool training activity.

How Long

How long will it take for the brownies to be ready? How much longer before the Jello will set? How long after lunch must I wait to go swimming? How long before dinner will be ready? "Soon" is not an answer; "later" isn't either; in a "minute" usually isn't. "I don't know" can instigate a tantrum! Two methods usually work: Use an oven timer to set the number of minutes a child has to wait. It will seem forever but at least it can be watched. Time is tangible then. Or draw a clock face on a cardboard with the hands pointed to the time it will be for dinner. "When the kitchen clock looks like this you may wash and come in to eat."

Washing before dinner was always a must! Sitting down to eat, the four year old suddenly hit his forehead and exclaimed, "Oh no!" "What!" came the responses round the table. "Oops, when I washed I forgot and also brushed my teeth!"

Sorting

If the child dries the dishes or removes them from a dishwasher, it is good practice to have him or her sort them in piles on the table or counter. All sorting, separating, and categorizing is important preschool training.

Pretend

- Silverware lined up into a long train
- Clothespin dolls sleeping in a loaf pan
- Spatulas turned into spacemen
- A pea pod for a boat

- Cooking pans upside down for houses or garages

Stacking   Storage containers, pots and pans, canned goods, and cereal boxes are perfect for stacking.

Rog: Look, Dad, I made a whole city on the kitchen floor while you were mixing the cake. What would make good skyscrapers, do you suppose?

Dad: How about standing the paper towel roller on its end and putting the wax paper and foil boxes on their ends next to it?

Listening   Can we keep very still and listen to the clock tick? Can we hear the tea kettle whistle when the water has boiled? Will the cats come running when the can opener signals their meal time? In one family the cats only come for their own dinner at exactly five o'clock. Any other can that is opened does not bring them running.

Temperature   Distinguish from hot and *too* hot—safety rules begin here. Distinguish from cold and *too* cold—holding an ice cube can cause frost burn. When some objects (butter, chocolate, jelly) are heated, they *melt*. When some things are put in the refrigerator they become hard (gelatin, butter) and in the freezer, *very* hard. A cake has to cool before it can be eaten. Warm cookies taste different from cold ones.

Steam is a good lesson when discussing "too hot." Draw attention to it coming from a tea kettle. Point to it above the coffee cup, the cereal bowl. A burnt tongue is the more painful way to learn this lesson.

Weights and Measures   Compare the weight of a five-pound bag of flour with a cup of flour. Compare the weight of a five-pound bag of potatoes with a single potato. Do tall cans feel heavier than short ones? Would a big turkey be heavier than a hamburger? Is a sponge heavier than a spoon? Tell them that biggest is not always heaviest.

Some objects take two hands to carry, others only one; some things take a strong man to lift, others even the child can handle. Ask, "will this be too heavy for you to carry? Are you big and strong enough to help me with it?" Let a child flex and show off a muscle. Being strong is a highly regarded attribute.

Vocabulary.   Ounces, quarts, pounds, half, quarter, gallon, bushel, pint, and half-pint will all be Greek out of context, but while measuring or ordering from the grocery, it is good to relate the word to the deed.

> Dad: I'll need a half-pound of ham and a half-pound of corn-beef. Look, Matt, how the needle on the scale moves as the deli man puts our cold cuts on his scale.

> Cathy: Can you help me carry in the milk? I bought a half-gallon this time because Mom said we're having company. But I only bought a pint of ice cream because the company is on a diet.

- "Why are you pinching the salt?", one child asks.

- "How much is a smidgeon or a speck? Daddy wants a speck more sugar in his tea."

- "Can I have a teensie bit more time to stay up?"

- "No, not an iota more!"

- "It simply took ages for them to come." "I know, it felt like forever!"

Magic   It is like magic when batter becomes a cake; powders dissolve with water into syrups; frosting turns pink or yellow with vegetable dye; purees come out of a blender; sparkling water makes a drink bubbly; a kernel becomes popcorn; and cabbage can be sauerkraut.

Origins   A child has no concept of the origin of food. What grows in the ground, comes from animals, and is manufactured? Try through stories, pictures, or field trips to bring this understanding to your child. Many companies permit such visits. Going to a farm or dairy will open a child to the gifts we receive from domestic animals. Although few children can express why, most children like one or two simple and easily identifiable foods on a plate and usually shun stews, chop sueys, or anything that is composed of several strange ingredients. Food should be something familiar. So familiarize your child with its origins.

"We get ham, bacon, and pork chops from a pig. The hens lay eggs for us. And the cow gives us milk," the teacher explained. "It wasn't giving it away," Betty retorted. "I saw the farmer *take* it."

Kitchen Kapers

A task accomplished gives a child satisfaction. Often adults have unreasonable expectations and give a small child something too difficult. More often they don't think of a child as a help, just a nuisance. "Don't bother me" are probably three more frequently used words than "I love you."

CHILD CHORES

- Wash and drain fresh produce.

- Set the table.

- Put sliced uncooked cookies on cookie sheet.

- Put away baked cookies.

- Grease tins for baking.

- Break up nuts or remove them from shells.

- Shell peas from pods.

- Snap string beans.

- Squeeze whipped cream from pressurized can onto Jello, puddings, ice cream.

- Put muffin liners in muffin trays.

- Measure raisins, nuts, chocolate bits, coconut.

- Crimp pie crust.

- Stir Jello.

- Toss salad.

- Arrange crackers and cheese for company.

- Add touches to hors d'oeuvres.

- Lap beaters and scrape the bowl.

- Wipe counters.

- Get out and put away supplies.

- Cut cookie dough with cookie-cutters.

- Spoon batter into muffin tins.

Gus would not eat raw carrots until his mother suggested he use the carrot sticks to make a decoration on his plate. Suddenly the carrots tasted better.

Sequence

Yesterday we made the Jello. *Today* we eat it. We mixed the cake *before*. We baked it *after*. *Today* we make the stuffed eggs. *Tomorrow* we will eat them. We have to beat the eggs *before* we add the flour. *Later* we put in the nuts.

Nutrition

What we eat helps us to grow healthy and strong. Green vegetables build our muscles and yellow vegetables are good for our eyes. Meat makes our blood better and milk works for our bones and teeth. Orange juice fights Mr. Cold Germ. Did you know that food has vitamins and each one is like a helper working for our health?

Dividing and Sharing

Mostly what a child sees is addition in the kitchen. The cook adds a little of this and that to make the recipe. Subtraction is when more and more is eaten away and little of the whole is left. But how does the cook know how to divide up the dish to feed the number of people who are eating? And how does the food stretch when a guest unexpectedly arrives?

Food Fancies for Flagging Appetites or Just for Fun

Why not dress up the child's plate in order to make the food more appetizing? All that is needed is imagination and color.

- To a dish of oatmeal: Add raisin eyes and mouth.

- Eggs, toast, and bacon: Bacon hair, toast ears, egg eyes, orange slice mouth.

- Pancakes: Raisin eyes, cherry/apple skin nose, apple slice mouth. (Or make pancakes into shapes and sizes: three sizes: a snowman, round and oblong, a dog, and crumbs.)

- Scrambled eggs: Arrange like a sun; use cheese strips for rays.

- Hot dog man: Cut off top, fry or bake; cuts make hot dog spread into a man, pin on top with toothpick. Cheese can be added for clothing. The roll can be the "house".

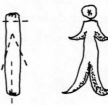

- Bread: Cut in shapes with a cookie-cutter or kitchen shears.
- Celery, carrots, radishes, apples: Celery hair, sandwich eyes, carrot nose, apple slice mouth.

Larrabee

- Radish: Roses or rosebud mouth.

- Carrots: Hair, nose.

- Celery: Hair, arms, legs, ears.

- Fruit: Mouths, hats, bow ties.

- Lettuce: Hair.

- Tomato: Mouth.

- Pickles: Eyes.

- Olives: Eyes.

FRAMED HAMBURGER FACE

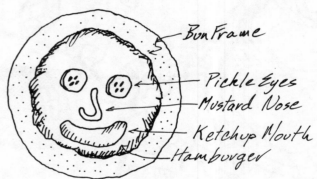

- Grilled cheese: Round bread covered with cheese tomato eyes, bacon mouth.

- Cold cut specials: Cut into shapes with cookie cutter. Use leftovers in omelets, soups, or ground up into sandwich spread.

Soupy Seas.   As much fun as it is to find alphabet letters in the soup, it is also fun to "fish" for carrots or noodles or bits of meat.

Pizza People.   "Mock" pizzas can be made by spreading tomato paste on halves of English muffins. Decorate to make faces with cheese bits for eyes, cold cuts for the mouth, etc.

Tinted Milk, Colored Potatoes.   Use maraschino cherry juice, for instance, to tint otherwise bland foods, such as cream or cottage cheese, milk, mashed potatoes.

Bubbles.   Small children can't resist using straws. When the bubble-blowing gets out of hand, it is time to remind them that straws are to be used for drinking, too.

Finger Foods.   It can't be stressed enough that motor coordination in young children is not as developed as in adults. Therefore table "manners," skillful use of forks and knives, ability to cut one's meat, eating from a plate that has three kinds of food on it are all difficult for toddlers. Put a few small pieces of cut-up meat, for example, on a plate and permit either finger-feeding ("Myself!" the little ones often cry) or fork-feeding. Toothpicks may also be used to simulate hors d'oeuvres. Eating one food at a time is sometimes less overwhelming than being expected to clean one's heaping plate.

COMPANY'S COMING

Preparation

Time is the most important ingredient in any well-laid plan. Whatever time you have allotted for preparation, when there is a toddler underfoot, double it. That may mean baking ahead, cutting down on other activities to conserve energy, serving cold meals on the party day. Expect the unexpected always.

The best defense is offense, so the all-of-a-sudden happenings cannot interfere with deadlines. For example, Sally spills tomato juice on her clothes five minutes before the doorbell rings. Have another clean outfit waiting "on the bench." While you are dressing, Billy has been playing with the silverware on the table. What a neat train they made! Allow enough time to set the scene again.

Hideaways for Special Days

Keep small toys hidden in a cabinet to emerge only on special days. This can be for company coming, holidays, or "we're-in-too-long" days. It can be a special company doll or cuddly animal who keeps the little one company on days a parent is more harried and less patient.

One mother viewed the company's arrival as a countdown for a bomb explosion. The food right, the house clean, the host and hostess dressed—all of this to be orchestrated serenely with the accompaniment of the usual toddler distractions. When the door opened she prayed that all the preparations were synchronized, but there was always that fleeting worry: did Chip pour the detergent in the john and would it bubble when it flushed? Would the crackers be nibbled on the tray or his clothes be undone upon the floor? She vowed she would never entertain until that little monster was at least twenty-one-years old.

Sitters and Neighbors

If possible engage extra help or another's helping hands before or during the party. Everyone would like a Mary Poppins to whisk the children away, but "seen but not heard" was a Victorian euphemism that does not happen any more. A tot can be brought in to meet the company and then taken by a sitter to play in his or her room. Perhaps nap time can immediately follow the introductions. Most likely the child will be happier if playing next door. Try

to work an exchange program with a neighbor and entertain your friends only when your neighbor is not.

Clean Up

"Who's coming?" some children automatically ask when housecleaning is in the offing. Letting little ones work involves them in the party. The smallest can dust table legs and chair rungs; while the taller ones can dust shelves and table tops. Children enjoy polishing silver and door brasses and making glass surfaces mirror bright.

The four year old was given two chores to help her mom. She could wipe the spice bottle with a damp cloth, and she could bathe the polished silverware in a bowl of hot water and dry them off. Soon she was chatting amiably with the bottles. She washed their "faces" (the caps) and then their tummies. "There, nice and clean," she said. Then she laid the silver out in "families." Each setting represented a family which she instructed to behave and "stay clean" while the company was here.

Finger Foods

Fortunately party food is often finger food, which kids find finger-lickin' good. Any bite size food is child size. Therefore, cheese cubes, carrot sticks, pretzels, olives, or slivers of cold cuts can be attractive to little ones. A child can help prepare hors d'oeuvres of alternating cheese and salami cubes on a toothpick, any of these stuck around a grapefruit or pineapple, precut carrot sticks stuck in pitted black olives, gherkin pickles rolled in a bologna "blanket," a ring of shrimp around the cocktail sauce, pretzel sticks piled like neat logs, rows of celery sticks, carrot sticks, or cucumber sticks.

Motivation

The best thing about company is company food. A motivation to "be good" is the hope of leftovers.

Josh looked up at his dad's boss with soulful eyes. "You won't eat up *everything*, will you?"

Decorations

• Name tags cut from old greeting cards or leftover wrapping paper.

• Holiday tags: wreaths, easter eggs, pumpkins with each guest's name.

• Napkins cut in lace shapes or gaily colored.

- Paper plates adorned with faces: good for picnics or barbecues.
- Crayon designs on paper cups.

Categories

Help your child learn about these go-togethers:

- salt and pepper
- sugar and creamer
- carving fork and knife
- punch bowl and cups
- ladle and tureen
- berries and cream
- tea and lemon
- rolls and butter
- soup and crackers
- chips and dips

Vocabulary Stretchers

So many new tasks and objects enrich a child's life at company time. Just as best behavior is warranted so is best china or silver. An ingenuous child will sometimes embarrass a parent by asking, "Hey, how come we're using all this good stuff tonight?" Some new words may be:

- slice and dice
- cubes and tubes
- sauce and gloss
- silver, chrome, pewter, brass
- gleam, shine, buff, hone, glisten, spray, arrange, select, order
- centerpiece

Trying hard to use grownup words for the grownup occasion, she asked the visitor for the biscuits, "Will you please pass the big tits?"

Dressing Distractions In the race to make everything come out at the same time and to present a serene face at the door, the age-old enigma is what to do with a toddler when one is dressing for the party?

1. Line up a row of Mom's high heels or Dad's big shoes and let him/her try them on. Shoes are the most fascinating item in any closet!

2. Permit him/her to put on own makeup or shaving cream given in a little kit of those no longer used. (If it doesn't bother you to introduce the child to the guests with the makeup on.)

3. For little boys who may have prejudices about wearing lady's makeup, let it be clown makeup.

4. Keep a supply of scarves and beads on hand, old nightgowns or party dresses that can become "ball gowns," old neckties, and sports coats for going to work. Then child and adult are both "dressing up."

5. "Rope off" (with chairs laid on their side) an area for the little one to play in (assuming he or she is too old for a playpen) with toys saved especially for this time.

6. Don't forget that perfumes, dusting powders, colognes, shaving lotions, and soaps-on-a-rope intrigue little ones. Allow as much scented stuff to fill the air while you are dressing as your nostrils will permit.

7. A child could sit in a shallow tepid tub of water and have a play bath while you dress or shave nearby. (Don't get splashed!) Remember never leave a child in a tub unattended!

Schedules Never forget the child's normal schedule on any hectic day when company is expected. If he or she regularly lunches at noon, and on this occasion won't until 2, expect a cranky child. If the little one is being allowed to stay up till dinner which is at 7:30 instead of 6, stave off starvation with small finger snacks.

It is harder to change sleeping patterns. If the child is about to drop off, tuck him or her in and tell the company they will meet sometime when your little one is old enough to stay up with adults.

Company's Arrived Alternatives are for the child to be introduced and whisked away, included, or ignored. *More accidents happen to preschoolers when their parents are distracted.* No little one can be forgotten even for "a moment." Since entertaining is for some people a particularly stressful and certainly a distracting time, it can not be said enough, please be certain the young child is carefully watched at this time.

How much can a child be included? How many thirty year olds enjoy talking to a three year old? How many three year olds are comfortable hosting a twelve year old? How much the child will be included ought to be decided ahead of time, and made clear to the child. Many parents want their children to be a part of a party; while others believe their friends left their own children home and need not be subjected to the host's. This is a matter of personal philosophy and it is good to have a policy on it.

Variations.   Beach, barbecue, picnic, cousins, clubs, and church events usually lend themselves to multi-age activities. Cocktails, formal sitdown dinners, the boss-is-coming, the minister-is-calling, frail Aunt Tessie and snippy Uncle Ted, the childless—these events or guests may not.

Mixers   When it is a mixture of ages such as cousins, grandparents, or whole families with assorted children, the event calls for mixer games.

Charades.   Keep them simple for the little ones like Little Miss Muffet, Jack be Nimble, and other nursery rhymes. Team the youngest with an older partner to "even" the odds.

Hot and Cold.   Treasure hunts require the leader to call out "hot" or "cold" as the players move near or far from the hidden object.

Treasure Hunts.   Use pennies, candy, raisins, nuts, or balloons and hide them preferably outside, in good weather, to keep the house in shape for the company.

Teams.   When playing any familiar game (e. g., ball, croquet, tag, hide-n-seek) take into consideration the handicap a preschooler faces and team him or her with a partner. The two players act as one in the scoring.

Manners Is there an adult anywhere in the world who does not coach a little one to "mind your manners" whether he or she is to be company or have some? Not only is the food or silver on display, but our most precious objects at these times seem to be our children! Best manners are taught by example and are best transmitted in daily situations. The adult who says "excuse me" to a child when called to the phone during a story period, or who remembers to say "please" and "thank you" when requesting or accepting an item, is most likely to have children who mimic this behavior.

"I remembered my pleases and thank you's," Stephen reported when he returned from the birthday party. "But I never got to use my excuse me's."

Don't Bother Me Moments or Instant Babysitters

MURDEROUS MOMENTS

1. Horrible headache
2. Tax time
3. Telephone musts
4. Day of the fair (four pies to bake)
5. Planning Scout banquet
6. Company's coming
7. Best friend has had surgery
8. You have had surgery

LIFE SAVERS

1. Water play; fill tub or sink and float items.
2. Make designs with noodles or spaghetti.
3. Pile up and then eat small finger foods: raisins, cold cereal, carrot sticks.
4. Pick a "to-be-played-with-at-special-times" item from a drawer.
5. Roll a ball back and forth to child, good while in bed or on the phone.
6. Let child shell peas from a pod or nuts from shells.

7. Turn a corner of room into special play area.

8. Engage an older child to watch your toddler in *your* home, thus freeing you for what you want to do.

9. Have a rocking chair and relaxing music available for you or your child.

10. Set a timer so the child can see when to bother and when not to.

11. Keep a supply of balloons handy.

RAINY DAYS

Cabin fever is a disease known to the occupants of Noah's Ark and parents of preschool children. Rain on a roof is a soothing sound, but when it keeps active youngsters confined, it is only good for farmers. Therefore, a wise adult saves certain objects and activities that are marked "rainy day fun." It is suggested that whatever household tasks can be suspended during the flood, they be put off for a "sunny day." Instead, direct your energy to supervising, refereeing, distracting, and making life more pleasant for all the shut-ins. The old refrain "rain, rain go away, come again some other day" never worked anyway!

Whether or not you grew up near a "grandma's attic," you ought to have the fixins for one. Acquire an old trunk (though an extra closet or packing case will certainly do) and stock it with imaginative dress-up clothes and props.

Costumes Second-hand shops, rummage sales, white elephant sales, and auctions are the niftiest places to shop for costumes. They may be dry cleaned or laundered, if there is concern about acquiring someone else's clothing. An old cape, for example, can be a stocking stuffer or birthday gift, while a gaudy necklace or flashy blouse a "queen's ransom" to a tot.

A good theatrical wardrobe should include:

- hats of every type (see "Hats" on p. 102)

- shoes of every type

- scarves

- canes

- spectacles of every type

- dad's old jackets, mom's old coats

- pipes

- wigs, mustaches (from joke shops)

- leftover cosmetics

- out-of-fashion costume jewelry

- black gum (to blacken out a tooth)

- mother's old party dresses (nighties or negligees; the fancier the better for ball gowns)

- a variety of purses and wallets

- an aluminum foil crown or two (some hamburger takeout places often give these away)

- a chopstick covered in foil for a wand

- any army surplus equipment that can be picked up cheaply

- (If you sew, do stitch up one or two velvet capes. No fairy tale is complete without one!)

- makeup (that comes off easily with cleansing cream) to make children look like pirates, Indians, princes, clowns, cowboys, princesses, hobos, and tatooed persons.

Houses   Imaginary houses:

- A behind-the-sofa sanctuary

- Under-the-bed cave

- A sheet-covered-cardtable haven

- A blanket-covered-big chair tepee

- Lying-down-kitchen-chairs fort

- An-empty-bathtub ocean liner

- Stacked-up-cartons treehouse

- A roped-off cellar clubhouse

- A darkened-corner spooky house (use only flashlights in it!)

- A clothes-line roped-off arena, rodeo, boxing ring

- A room partitioned with blankets on a clothes line-anything

Vehicles   Homemade vehicles:

- A row of chairs can become a train.

- An upturned table can become a boat.

- An upside-down overstuffed chair can become an airplane.

Listening Have them stretch out on their stomachs and listen to records or tapes. Cuddle in a big chair or big bed and listen to stories from parents' childhood, look at picture books, be told the old favorite fairy tales. Sing along in rounds or fill in a missing word as the leader sings. Learn a simple square dance; clap hands to the rhythm of it. Listen to the rain on the roof or window. Talk about what makes the thunder. Beat a real or homemade drum whenever a thunder clap hits the house. (Who's afraid? Not me! Well, a little? You bet!)

Puppets Puppets can be made from clothespins, socks, pipe cleaners, tongue depressors, spoons, bottles, sticks and wire, a child's finger (paint faces on each one), old gloves (do same as fingers), styrofoam, pens, pencils, potatoes, and apples.

A Rainy Day Song "Eensie weensie spider went up the water spout. Down came the rain and washed the spider out. Out came the sun and dried up all the rain. Then eensie weensie spider went up the spout again."

Does your child know what a water spout is? A spider? Time to take out dictionaries, encyclopedias, or a book of knowledge and look at pictures.

Construction A construction project that can take days and days is ideal for a long rainy siege. Use toy logs, bricks, Leggos, Tinker Toys, blocks, playing cards, dominoes, or any of these in a combination. Let it fill a room or the whole apartment or all of the downstairs of a house. If electric trains are available, lay the track throughout the entire living room. (Wow! Anything goes when it rains!)

A budding preschool architect would fill his entire bedroom with artifacts he created from his imagination. Scraps and leftovers of every kind became a replica of a real object to him. One day he turned that room into a movie set, attempting to reproduce a Walt Disney movie he had just seen. No one could enter that special place of his imagination, as it was off-bounds to adults. When he grew up, he did indeed become an architect.

Puzzles Intricate picture puzzles are too difficult for little people. Wooden ones with big pieces are easier to handle and perceive. However, adults often relax with a multi-piece puzzle that takes days or weeks to complete. A small child will enjoy watching an adult complete the pictures and will sharpen his or her own perception skills as the picture emerges.

Homemaking Rainy days can provide an opportunity for a course in the domestic arts:

- Learning to dust table or chair legs (where a child can easily reach), cellar or attic steps, book shelves and/or books.

- Learning to stir the Jello or pudding, decorate a cake, cut cookies.

- Learning to hammer a nail, use a screwdriver, sort screws and nails in jars.

- Learning to sort, fold, and put away laundry.

- Learning to polish silver, doorknobs, a mirror.

- Learning to put silverware on the table.

- Learning to use peeler on carrots, cucumbers.

- Work can be play to a child and help make him or her feel an important part of the family.

Some "helping" a parent doesn't need! One four year old brought the garden hose into the house through his bedroom window and "watered" the flowers on his wall! Another two year old "cooked soup", stirring the water in the toilet bowl with a kitchen spoon. When his brother flushed the spoon down, the toddler's fright set his toilet training back a year!

Safety Make a conscious effort to instruct a youngster on safety rules. Rainy day time is a good time for this instruction. Explain why the stove is too hot to go near when food is cooking; why cleaning fluids and medicines are kept up and away from little fingers; why electric sockets should not be poked into or electric wires played with. Explain that a telephone is not a toy, but that a toy telephone is fun to use for pretending games. Explain what is too sharp, too cold, too hot, too thin, too delicate, and whatever is too valuable for play. Perhaps a tour of the house can be made with this in mind, or a game made up with labels with a huge "X" stuck on the "don't touch me" items.

Observing   Rainy days are excellent days for observing:

- The design on a table cloth or a lacy paper doily.
- The pattern of the raindrops on a window.
- Puddles filling the low spots outdoors.
- The sway of the trees in the storm. (Is it a dance of the branches?)
- Birds lined up outdoors on a telephone wire.

Photo Albums   Almost nothing intrigues a child as much as looking at old family pictures. Either bring out old albums, if you have them, or sort pictures to be placed in an album together. If colored slides make up your picture library, darken the room for home movies. Children especially like to see themselves when they were babies and what their parents looked like as children.

Judy was amazed at the picture of her granny with her daddy as a kid. "Gee you used to be bigger than my daddy when he was a boy, but look, now he is bigger than you," she observed. "Gosh, granny, what made you shrink?"

Just for Moms and Dads   Many people put off ironing or mending tasks for a rainy day. But these are lonely and often boring jobs. Instead, invite a neighbor to iron with you. Set up the boards across from each other and iron while you visit. The children can play happily in the next room until everyone takes a cookie break.

Cut and Paste   Although small fingers rarely have the coordination for precision cutting, they love making a grand mess of cutting up things and this helps them develop that coordination. Therefore provide objects that are easy to cut and do not require following the lines. Use only blunt end scissors.

Paste rope or yarn to cardboard. It is okay for it to be a picture, design, or just a mess. Cut up old catalogs or magazines and paste into a scrapbook. Paste discarded buttons to a cardboard in a pattern or design. (Use heavy duty glue for objects heavier than paper.)

Paste small jar lids to a cardboard. Cut and paste sheets of colored construction or crepe paper, just for the color and the good feeling of squishing paste. A recipe for paste is one-half cup flour, a pinch of salt and enough water to make it sticky.

Punch and Lace   Adults can punch holes near the edges of old greeting cards, shirt boards or any piece of cardboard. The child can use long shoelaces to lace a design.

Get Ready or Finish Up   Time is on your side on a rainy day. You might want to measure for the hem on your daughter's new dress, try out a special new recipe, clean out a closet, repair the camping tent, try on last winter's boots. (Do they still fit?)

See It   Let your child use a magnifying glass to look at spoons, plants, vegetables, etc. He will be amazed at what he sees. Give him a mirror to make faces at; or a piece of mosquito netting or old translucent curtains to hold over his face. Then he will see the world through lines and haze.

Hats   • *Top hats*—Deep plastic containers put on head upside down.

- *Chinese hats*—Large funnel upside down.

- *Fashionable bonnet*—Decorate a paper plate, with crayons or paints, or paste on bits of colored paper. Make hole on opposite sides, put ribbons through holes. Tie hat under chin.

- *Stocking hats*—Old socks can be knotted together and pulled over head to make a hat.

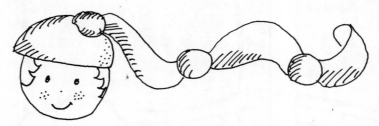

- *Flower pot hats* (plastics only please)—Child picks any size pot and decorates it with stick-ons, paste and paper designs, water color paints, and markers. Adult punches holes (can opener will do this) for ribbons to tie hat on.

- *Saucepan helmets*—Pan over head.

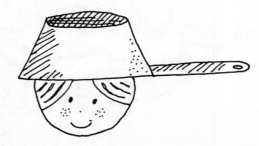

- *Old hats*—It's fun just to put on mother's or grandmother's old hat and pretend.

- *Turban hats*—Wrap a towel around and around and tuck in.

- *Bridal veil*—Drape old curtain over head and let flow out behind (attach with hairpins).

- *Newspaper hats*—Fold newspapers (folded sheet-double sheet) in half. Fold ends of fold into middle. Fold up ends on each side. Hats can be colored with crayons, paint, or markers if desired.

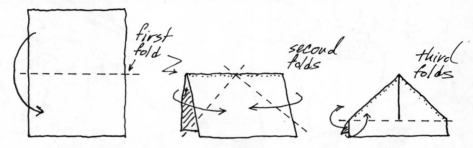

- *Bandana hats*—Tie scarfs in different ways to make a variety of hats.

Recipes for Artwork

The kitchen is a veritable art studio. Raisins, dates, nuts = designs. Using cookie cutters on cold meats, cookie dough, or bread slices = teddy bears, valentines, or snowmen. Apple slices, orange segments, carrot curls, and celery pieces = more designs. And after your child makes the designs he can eat it! Also juice and water = finger paint; and flour and water and a pinch of salt = paste.

With big pieces of paper and a large pencil or crayon plus a round pie tin or square cake pan, your child can begin to trace a shape. Help him learn how to hold paper with one hand as he traces with other. Let him use whichever hand he chooses (he may alternate) and remember that the tracings will be primitive because young hands don't have much motor control.

Empty boxes, old bags, bits of string or ribbon, empty tin cans, and cardboard tubes can be cut, colored, pasted, or painted. What can your child make?

Macaroni pieces, nuts in the shell, dry cereals, and beans can be pasted or glued on paper plates to make designs such as wreaths and flowers. The parent can cut a circle out of the middle first. When color sprayed, they are really pretty. Spray it gold and hang up for holidays.

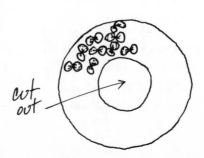

Paper plates can be made into faces, clocks, puppets, hats, or masks. Paste on a tongue depressor for handle. (Young children don't like "eye" holes.)

HALLOWEEN
MASK

Pull an old sock over a bowl of large spoon and tie around handle with a ribbon to make a spoon puppet. With magic markers face features can add realism. Silverware can be lined up to make a long train. A clothespin doll can take a nap in a loaf pan bed. Two large cooking spoons or spatulas can become outerspace people touring the earth. A bunch of magnets make pictures on the

refrigerator. Buttons, toothpicks, poker chips also make designs. (Be sure the child is old enough not to put these in his mouth.)

Pipe cleaners and straws bend into interesting shapes. Egg cartons become caterpillars, butterflies, and flowers. (Be sure to add color.) Cupcake papers make doll hats, flowers, and nut baskets, when pasted on a paper plate for a party dinner.

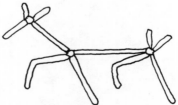

Let your child use a rotary beater and whip up one cup soap flakes with one cup water. He will have a thick mass that can be molded into shapes. A sponge tied around with a kerchief becomes a doll. Knot the kerchief and let it hang down as a skirt. Knot and hang 2 kerchiefs to cover back as well as front. A small measuring cup upside down can become a lady bug or a turtle. The handle is the tail. Add marking chalk or nontoxic water paints.

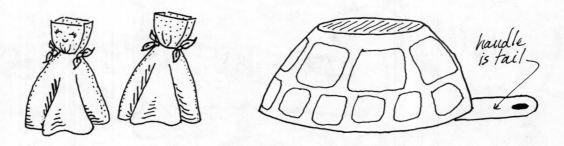

Using the bristles on a scrub brush as hair, wrap an old rag around the handle and pin it together. Now you have a teenager or maybe Uncle Alfred (if he is one of those lucky older men with abundant rather than nonexistent hair).

SAND AND WATER

Fun in the Sand

Nobody needs to tell a small child how soothing it is to let sand slip over one's fingers, to dig one's toes into it, to bury one's whole body, letting only a small head shine above it. Mothers and fathers discover early on that water, too, has this soothing effect and use it wisely to calm or distract overactive youngsters. Not everyone has access to sandy beaches or shores. Making opportunities for children to work with sand and water are often one way an adult can expose a little one to these tactile experiences. A sandtable in a corner of a room, a sandbox in a yard or a basement in the winter, access to a kitchen or bathroom sink, and plenty of squeezable plastic bottles and containers will provide some of the most relaxing moments your youngster can have.

HOLES

Depth, displacement, amounts, comparisons of density and dampness make any hole an ever-fascinating science experiment. Compare the amount of water in a muffin tin to the amount in a large hole of sand. How many pails of water does it take to fill that large hole? Will the next hole take more water? Less? What happens to the water in the hole? Where does it go?

STICK ART

Draw pictures in the sand with a stick. Use twigs, shells, seaweed, or leaves to decorate the picture. Sun rays, hair on a stickman, blades of grass can all be made. How artistic can you get?

A family spent all of a late afternoon decorating the empty beach. Everyone pitched in to create the beautiful sand mural. Sadly they watched the tide come and take it away to sea, their picture as fragile as the joy it took to create it.

MAPPING

A map in the sand is a simple way to begin to teach the skill of mapping. Draw a familiar landmark such as the school, store, church, and then a line to the house where you live. Draw in the streets and other landmarks of the neighbor-

hood. A child can trace the route with a stick or his finger. Make it *very simple* and increase the difficulty as the child shows willingness to learn.

DAMS

Simple construction projects in the sand demand an introduction to dams. Hold the water and let it out. A hole in a dam can be made and blocked with a stone demonstrating simple engineering on a primary level.

BRIDGES

Dig tunnels under the sand or lay large shells or shovel handles over a water trench and a child will have a bridge. What must he do to make his bridge strong enough not to cave in?

TREASURE HUNTS

Tales of hidden pirate treasure trigger other treasure hunts. One member of the group should bury a shiny rock, piece of seaweed, or other designated "treasure." Where there is salt water, "sea-glass," rough edges rubbed off by the sea, are genuine treasures almost any child would like to collect. The treasure hunters can be told when they are getting "warm," as they near the buried "loot."

TACTILE LETTERS

The child uses his fingers to trace letters and numbers in the sand. He or she is getting the "feel" of the figure. Similar to Braille for the blind, this is an important path to learning for the sighted as well.

CASTLES

Castles are limited only by the limits of an imagination and are best constructed in a group effort. That way even the youngest child can enjoy the fruits of his labor with the pleasure of a "spectacular" construction project.

Drip Castles. Great decorations to add a touch of "gingerbread" to any construction is the drip of wet sand upon the dried castle. It will roll down and dry in attractive patterns, similar to frosting on a cake.

SAND ANGELS

Place the child's head on a towel so it won't get sandy, and ask her to swing her arms and legs back and forth in the sand to make angel's wings. Variations are building a tail around the child's feet to resemble a mermaid, outlining the body with a stick and comparing the sizes of several children, outlining the body and taking away a part at a time, and asking the child to identify the fingers, elbow, knee. (A good way to teach the parts of the body.)

VEHICLES

Boats, trains, planes, or any other vehicle can be built out of sand. Make three-dimensional seats so that the builder can also "ride" in the completed project. A number of twigs and sticks stuck in the "dashboard" adds to the impressiveness of the structure. Add plastic lids and any shiny stones or shells to make an all-out space ship. Where there are tides, put it just below the high water line and see how long it can withstand the waves.

RACES

One line drawn in the sand is the starting line, another the finish. Don't make the distances too far for short legs, but extend the distance of the race as the child seems ready for it. It will help to leave one "race track" intact when you establish a longer one, so the child can see how much further he or she is running on the second track. (These are races, then, that a child is running against himself, rather than another child.) Broad jumping, hopping, giant steps, add to the racing fun.

WET OR DRY

Sand and hand go together. Ask him whether sand is wet or dry, rough or smooth, pebbly, grainy, mushy, or drippy? What language will your little one use to describe the feeling?

SAND DIALS

For the child who seems ready to grasp the concept of time draw a circle in the sand and place a stick in the center. As the shadow falls, so will it resemble the long hand of the clock. Try to compare the picture in the sand with a real watch.

Draw another circle in the sand. Place the child in the center. Let him dramatize a clock by using one hand for the big hand, the other for the short one. Can he move his hands around the clock and let the rest of us guess what time it is?

BAREFOOT IN THE SAND

Strong ankles and firm arches can be the result of walking barefoot in the sand. It takes greater muscle control to walk in deep sand, i.e., dunes, and thus builds up young feet.

BAKERY

Use cookie cutters to make "mud pies," and any other containers, lids, pots, or muffin tins to set a child up in the sand bakery business. Broken shells and stones are the nuts or cherries to top off any concoction. The rest is up to the imagination!

SAND GAMES

These include freeze, four square, red light, frisbee, giant steps, ring a round a rosy, hopscotch, catch, rattle snake, tag, blindman's bluff, red rover, and any game that ends with falling down in the soft sand!

TOYS

A collection of construction toys comes in handy at the beach, sandbox, or sand table. Kitchen sifters, strainers, funnels, and measuring cups are a welcome addition.

MEMORY STRETCHERS

Smooth a stretch of sand. Draw a geometric figure such as a square, circle, triangle, or rectangle in the sand and wipe it off. Have the child remember the figure and draw it with a stick in the sand. Repeat with two figures or make a row of shapes. Let the shapes become more complicated such as a hexagon, parallelogram, etc. The drawings can represent stick-people moving in either a left or right direction. Add details to the pictures as attention span of the child increases. Make up stories to go with the pictures.

TIC TAC TOE, SQUIGGLES

Many pencil and paper games can be adapted to the sand. For example, squiggles where one person starts a design and another person completes it in any way he wishes. In tic tac toe, take turns putting O's and X's in spaces. First person to make three in a line wins.

FOOTPRINTS/HANDPRINTS

Every child likes to compare his or her size to that of a grownup.

Footprints.   Compare all the footprints of both humans and animals. Go to the beach early and find the path crabs make, the herringbone marks of the sandpiper, or the paw prints a dog might have left behind.

Pairs. Dad or mom can walk in parallel rows barefoot on the sand and the children can do the same. How many *pairs* of footprints? Initiate an understanding of the concept of pairs.

Fingerprints. Smooth the sand and press your hand upon it. Compare the shapes and sizes of each handprint. In damp sand, the fingerprints are more apt to show clearly. In mud that hardens to clay, these handprints can be kept and saved.

Each person in the world has a unique fingerprint/footprint. It tells you who the person is, like a picture of your face. Newborn babies are footprinted so that they can't become mixed up with one another. Police can use fingerprints to tell who a person is. Sometimes these pictures and fingerprints are posted on the walls of post offices. These are called "wanted men," or "wanted women." Doesn't it seem strange that a *fingerprint/footprint* can tell someone who you are?

BAS RELIEFS

Some children are frightened to be buried, although it is only to the neck. Do it with acceptance of the child only! It may be more fun to bury an adult and build him or her into a mermaid, whale, seagull, fish, horse, cow, sheep, pig, lobster, jet plane, King Neptune (don't forget a crown), or whatever your imagination dictates!

Fun in the Water INDOORS

Place canvas on the floor next to the tub or under the bathroom sink or in front of the kitchen sink. Or place a basin (the size of a baby tub is good) on a table and lay the canvas under it. Pin a towel around the child's neck or let him or her play in a bathing suit indoors, if the house is warm enough to permit it. Worries about wetness should be eliminated before the activity. Getting wet can be relaxing. It can also be too stimulating. Splashing each other, however, is strictly forbidden. Running water from a faucet is also against the rules for this is a waste of water. Best is the freedom a child feels "cooking" or "experimenting," measuring, pouring from one container to another, spraying from spray bottles such as those used for washing windows and getting oneself wet *without guilt*. Even the child who hates to wash will play with water!

Outdoors or indoors, boats can be made from folded paper, leaves, seed pods, blocks of wood or cork, sticks, lily pads (frogs sail on them), logs, seaweed, half a tennis ball, plastic containers, shells, jar lids.

Aunt Ruth: You know the story about the owl and the pussycat who set out to sea in a big green pea?

Charles: Yeah?

Aunt Ruth: Well, if I hunt up some "boats," do you want to use your little men or Barbie and Ken dolls and set them out to sea in the bathtub?

Charles: Yeah!

SPONGES

Never discard an old sponge! They make wonderful water toys when cut in shapes. Usually in assorted colors, they are bright and soft, but what is best, they are "squeezy," a wonderfully good feeling to a child.

BAGGIES

Fill with water small plastic bags used for sandwiches. It is better to knot the ends, rather than use the twisted metal closures that come in the package, because these sometimes have exposed wire and can scratch a child's hands. The filled bags are fun to bounce around in a sink of water.

TEMPERATURE

Bowls of water are a good way to test and teach the concept of varying temperatures. "I am going to take your temperature" is an expression nearly every child hears often, but what does it mean to a child, other than it will tell if he or she is sick? A simple way to show this to a child is to place four bowls of water in front of him. One should have ice in it and the hottest should be just hot enough to be safe to the touch. Vocabulary like "tepid," "lukewarm" can be introduced as well, and boiling and freezing can be explained also.

STACKING

Buckets or pails come in assorted sizes. They can be stacked by graduation to make a tower or can be fit inside each other. Learning the gradations of size is an important early lesson in geometry. Measuring spoons and cups are similar tools for learning.

FLOATING AND SINKING

What will float? What will sink? Try different items such as leaves, nuts, full containers, and containers with holes. A child likes to pretend to be cooking.

Raw macaroni will float in the water and makes the cooking more interesting. When fingers become wrinkled, it is time for water play to end. In the outdoors, *never leave a child who is near water out of your sight!*

BALLS

Whatever ball game can be played on land can usually be played in the water: catch, roundrobin, basketball (using a floating object for a basket), dodgeball, and keep-a-way.

MOATS

Construction is so specialized these days. While one group is building the castle, could another create the moats? Make this another opportunity for vocabulary enrichment as well:

Once upon a time, there was a wicked king. He built the fanciest castle in all the land. But he was afraid the people would be jealous and come and take away his treasures. So to protect himself he built a *moat* around his castle. This separated his home from the town. Then he put a *drawbridge* across it. He could drop it down when he wanted to ride on his fine horse or go for a drive somewhere in his fine *coach*. When he wanted to be left safely alone, he could *draw* the bridge back up again. This is not the same as drawing a picture or a horse drawing a wagon behind it. It is done with ropes and *pulleys*. Let me show you a simple way this is done with a stick and string. Maybe someday we'll see a drawbridge raised for a tall boat to sail safely under the bridge.

BEACH COLLECTIONS

Many objects can be collected at the beach: sea glass, pebbles, shells, feathers, driftwood, sand dollars, cat-tails, marsh grass, bayberries, rocks, and any flora that can be dried for arrangements.

Mud Psychiatrists offer many theories about the therapy of mud. Some feel a child who has been toilet trained too early or too harshly will benefit from the freedom of playing with mud. Others say that a repressed child who is made to feel that getting dirty is "bad" will also benefit from the mess of mud. All we know is that mud is another tactile experience, cool, soothing, squishy, and different from either sand or water. Mudpies and children go together. Hundreds of juvenile bakeries have gone into business using mud for their main ingredient. It doesn't stain clothes and can easily be washed off floors. However, no matter how tastefully decorated, it should not be eaten!

COOKIE CUTTERS

Cookie cutters should be as much a staple in the sandbox or toy box as the kitchen. They can be used on playdough or clay as well as mud. They can tell a picture story, similar to the way the Egyptians used hieroglyphics.

Teacher: Once upon a time there was a dog, a cat, and a horse on a farm. Can you make them for me with your cookie cutter? At night they would look at the moon and stars. Can you make them for me with your cookie cutter?

FRACTIONS

Cutting mudpies in halves and quarters teaches whole, parts of wholes, and simple fractions. It is also the introduction to telling time.

PHENOMENA

Some mud hardens into clay. Some mud doesn't. Leave something made of mud to dry in the sun. How long will it take to become hard? Will the color change? What color is wet mud? Dry mud? When it is very hard, can you paint on what you have made?

The Pueblo Indians who live in the Southwest part of our country use the kind of mud that hardens to make their bowls and jugs. They paint them with bright colors. They even make their homes with it. Perhaps some day you will learn how to make a bowl or jug from this kind of mud (clay) and if you do, you will be known as a *potter*.

SHOPPING TRIPS

Shopping can certainly be a drag when little ones tag along. If you can't lick it, join it, and make shopping a learning experience for both of you. By involving your child in the purpose and scope of the shopping, you have a partner to share decision-making with.

Why Are We Shopping?

"We have to go shopping today," an adult says. The child may ask if it is for groceries? Is it for a quick pickup or a long afternoon of selecting, sorting, standing in lines and waiting, waiting, waiting? Is it to buy a present for Aunt Martha? Will it include some new clothes (and maybe a new toy) for the child? Will it be for food and will he or she have any input? (This is a good time to discover what kind of television advertising is making its pitch to the youngest consumer in the family.) Although it is impossible to convey the concept of time, it may be possible to compare the quality of it. Shopping for food is less tedious usually than other kinds of errands. Try to establish the purpose of the day before you are faced with that whining, "Wanna go home. . . ."

Where?

Shopping malls are designed as much for recreation as consumption. If it is one that features a hot pretzel stand or cotton candy machine or automated rides, use these as incentives to make the trip attractive. Try to shop where there are available drinks and bathrooms. Use a focal point from a former trip to whet the child's anticipation.

"We are going to Jordan Marsh to buy new dishes, Butch."
"Don't wanna."
"You like shopping there!"
"Don't."
"But that's the place that has the little chairs and table for children to sit at and color while their moms are picking out the new things. Remember?"
"Okay."

Behavior   "The best-laid plans of mice and men . . ." ought to be changed to parents and children. It is good to instruct a child about expected behavior before entering a store. If it is to be a positively *don't touch* place, be firm in your intentions. Some places are more "touchable." Try to teach the differences, but don't expect this to be an easy lesson for a child to grasp!

The fantastic multi-tiered wedding cake was marred by a wide swath cut through the frosting. Evidence of the culprit was clear. Denying she had touched the cake, she wore its sweet frosting across her sweetly "innocent" face.

Participation   Children are usually overlooked on a shopping trip until their behavior attracts attention, usually the negative kind. By including a little one as a companion and partner, you raise his or her self-esteem and lessen the opportunities for inappropriate behavior. Assign a job:

- Finding—looking out for the cereals, cookies, ice cream.

- Filling—the child puts the items in the basket or wagon.

- Opinion-giving—the blue scarf or the red one for his teacher?

- Carrying—carefully handling the gift-wrapped present.

- Supervision—keeping an eye on the baby while Mom or Dad ducks quickly into a drug store, magazine stand, ice cream parlor.

Shopping Wonderland   Busy adults take for granted the wonders that abound for little people. Allow time for discoveries and discussions about such wonders as escalators, elevators (Why do the lights pop on and off above the door? How do you keep the doors from closing on you? Does the elevator ever get stuck between floors?), conveyor belts, computerized checkouts, burglar alarms, sprinkler systems, automatic sliding doors, check-cashing machines, pinball machines, telephone booths, vending machines, bike racks, loading platforms, buzzers, signals, flashing lights, bells, and gongs. The list is endless.

The pyramid of tomato soup cans was irresistible. While his mother stood at the checkout, he cautiously pulled a can from the geometric center. The crash of rolling cans in every direction was one of his most triumphant moments of destruction!

Furs   If no zoo or museum is in the area, visit the fur department of a clothing store. This is an eyes-on rather than a hands-on field trip. The assortment of furs is a quick and easy way to see how animals keep themselves warm.

Food   How many preschoolers understand where milk, eggs, steak, and hamburger come from? Use the food shopping expedition to explain the origins of their favorite food, such as drumstick from chicken or turkey, ham from a pig, etc.

> Peter: "Where does peanut butter come from, huh?"
>
> His older brother: "Grows from peanut butter plants, dummy!"

Mikki became a 3-year-old vegetarian when she realized her lamb chops came from a "little lambie."

Bread   The staff of life comes in an array of products. Expose young children to the variety of wheat types, and roll the words honey, bran, molasses, rye, Syrian, and French-stick around on your tongues. The names are as delicious as the breads.

Bakeries   Busy bakeries often rely on a number machine for fairness. Customers feast their eyes on the showcase displays while waiting their turn. Not only does this teach a child an example in patience, but it is an excellent way to help him or her become acquainted with numbers as in amounts "six cupcakes please," and also in order, "we are fifth in line."

Scales and Measures   Never overlook an opportunity to compare instruments and words of measurement. The vocabulary will long be a mystery (quarts, pounds, ounces, liters, gallons) but looking at these items will lay the foundation for future math concepts.

Money   Provide the child with a small purse and small change. (Tuck the purse or wallet in your own pocket or pocketbook if you fear it will become lost.) Nothing makes a child feel more grown-up than the use of his or her own money. It is best that it be spent at the end of the trip, to give the child a goal for which to be "good."

Clothes Shoes may be the only item of clothing a child will like to buy for himself. Trying on Mom's or Dad's is one of the earliest manifestations of roleplaying and is probably a symbolic attempt to "fill a grown-up's shoes." But buying other garments can be a terrific bore. If this is so with your youngster, make every effort to buy clothes without the child. It is the trying-on procedure that is the most trying for everyone. Instead, take along a shirt or pair of p.j.'s that fit and either buy more of the same size or some of the next. It may be better to buy and return than face the temper tantrums some children spring in dressing rooms.

Looking, Looking, Looking Looking is a requisite for shopping. It is part of the selection process, automatic to an adult. Teach a child to *look*.

"I am looking for some new green towels for the bathroom. Can you look for something green?"

"I am looking for the salesperson to ring up this sale. Can you be looking, too?"

"I am looking for a store that sells garden tools. It has a big red sign with a garden on it. Can you find it before I do?"

Check-out lines can be fun too. They provide time for counting people or things and for watching what is going on.

Strays Separation may or may not cause the child anxiety, but it certainly causes it for the person responsible for the stray. The adventurer will think the adult got lost (Where did you go, Mommy?), while the timid will panic. In either case, it is important to teach a child about the Lost and Found departments of most stores, and read aloud at an early age the delightful picture book, "Lucy McLocket," by Phyllis McGinley, which deals with this theme.

In crowded places, dress the toddler in either a bright hat, scarf, or jacket so that he or she can be easily spotted.

If the child is too young to give his or her name and telephone number, pin identification on the outer clothing. (In stuffy stores, remove coats and hats and put the identification on the shirt or jersey. Overheated children are cranky children.)

The four year old was paged on the loudspeaker of the large store. At last he was discovered and brought to "Lost and Found." A stern clerk suggested certain and devastating punishment for the incurable wanderer. "Tie this rope to his hand and to yours," she instructed the child's mother. "That will curb him once and for all." But the child was irrepressible. "Look at me, I'm an escaped prisoner," he gleefully shouted through the store. The punishment was merely grist for his active imagination.

Wiggles and Pushes and Screams and Tears

Why do these occur? Little people wear out and get tired of seeing only legs and more legs. Little people get tired of just standing or just sitting. Little people get hungry and thirsty, bored and sleepy. Shopping is best done with a full stomach and a rested body, for BOTH of you.

A toy or snack tucked away for the trying moment, and a trip to the rest rooms before a clean-up demands it are good hints to avoid potential problems.

PETS AND PRESCHOOLERS

Who said no home was complete without a pet? As if having a preschooler isn't enough, having a pooch or kitten will not necessarily make it happily ever after! Some of the good old American myths are: 1) every child needs a pet; or 2) as long as we're having children, why not raise pets and kids together; or and the granddaddy myth of them all; 3) it'll teach the kids responsibility.

Responsibility. One of the hardest aspects of childrearing is knowing what are realistic expectations. Very young children have a hard enough time being responsible for their behavior without the additional burden of having to remember to care for an animal. No child up to the age of ten will remember to walk, feed, or groom an animal *consistently.* Adults who expect not to assume the responsibility for an animal can also expect to be disappointed. The child who lets a parent down this way then has the added burden of being a "bad" child. Thus, instead of the pet becoming a growth experience it becomes a guilt-inducing one.

Companionship. Once the novelty of a small animal wears off, the child may feel the pet is a nuisance. Since most young children are not skilled in gentleness, they inadvertently handle animals improperly. Well-meaning squeezes and overcuddling can lead to irate bites and scratches. The fear of animals can result, the reverse of the intended relationship.

Sibling Rivalry. It works both ways. The family that has had an animal before a child may discover the animal becoming jealous of the new addition. The child, however, who must compete for attention when the new puppy or kitten requires parenting may also resent the competition. It is important to regard both young creatures as toddlers, and *if you are prepared to raise twins,* then have a preschooler and a pet at the same time! *Never take a creature that belongs to the*

wild (raccoon, skunk, squirrel, bird) in as a pet. It is not usually geared toward civilization and when the novelty of having it wears off, it will then be unable to cope again in the wild.

Allergies.   Many children are allergic to cats, dogs, horses, or birds. Such allergies can be both debilitating and detrimental to the child's development. Sometimes these allergies do not become apparent until the pet has been in the house for several weeks. Coughing, sneezing, and wheezing are common allergic reactions but allergies can also be masked as continual colds, irritability, listlessness, itching, stomach aches, or some other problem.

SICK-IN-BED BLUES

Sick can mean anything from a grumpy day of sniffles to a prolonged convalescence. While only a physician's orders should be followed during a severe illness and recovery period, it is hoped that a measure of common sense and an extra spoonful of love will "help the medicine go down." This is when a child's short attention span is even shorter, when even well-intentioned cheering-up can be overtiring, and when most out-of-sorts people (young and old) want someone nearby and caring.

The following are tips to brighten the sickroom.

1. A cold pitcher of water by the bed for dry throats. Use nonbreakable bendable straws as they do in hospitals. Most children think straws are great and they do prevent spills.

2. Extra fluffy pillows. The child who must stay in bed may enjoy sinking into them or building them up into a fort.

3. A pet doll or stuffed animal to cuddle.

4. Frequent changes of sleepware. Give a back rub or sprinkle with talc. It will make the patient feel more comfortable, and pampered too.

5. Frequent changes of bedding. Children will wet the bed or spill food more often when they don't feel well.

6. A damp washcloth in a plastic bag or the handiwipe dampened papers that spring from a box can be refreshing as well as cleansing.

7. Pretty ribbons to tie a little girl's hair up from her face. Fevers demand cooling down. Spray her with cologne from an atomizer.

8. Toys that take up little space on a bed and require little concentration, such as a kaleidoscope or colorforms.

9. Wearing dad or mom's robe, pajama top, or sheer negligee.

10. Flowers, dry arrangements, or a mobile nearby for the child who must lie still.

11. Pictures on the wall changed daily. Animal pictures are especially good.

12. Window shades to half point, dim lights, soft-colored bulbs in the lamps.

13. Bed trays.

14. Things to suck, such as popsicles, lollypops, or cherry drops.

15. Pills in applesauce if the child is too young to swallow pills.

16. Fancy foods (see page 83 on fancy foods) for flagging appetites, e.g., sandwiches cut in shapes and one food at a time, such as a baked potato, or small bowl of soup.

17. Rocking on a lap or rocking chair, a heavenly and reassuring rhythm.

18. Oven timer set to go off for when it is time for you to return.

19. Dinner bell to signal need for company.

20. A bottle for the toilet-trained boy.

21. Record player or tape playing favorite songs softly.

22. Most important is You, the mother, father, babysitter, foster parent, grand-parent. Your time for a little talk, story, song, or book can make a sick child feel much better. Sick-in-bed-blues requires time taken from routine work and is as important as any prescription a doctor writes.

Tales All children want to hear about when they were little or when the storyteller was little. But sickness limits the listening time. Keep it short and stop at an exciting time. Say, "now you rest awhile and when I come back I'll tell you what happened after that."

Cages If the child is required to stay in bed, build a cage around him to help him remember. Use chairs with backs placed against the bed or place a bright ribbon along its sides from bedpost to bedpost.

Shadow Plays By placing a light behind the child, he or she can make forms with the hands that will cast shadows. What fun to make the figures dance on the wall!

Tray Ornaments   Give the bedtray a pick-me-up: a nosegay of flowers, a puppet stuck in an empty cup, a clay figure with a sad face, a homemade get-well card.

When the Parent Is Sick   Let the child help you. This will give him something to do and help him handle the childhood apprehension of "will you get well soon, mommy?" Very young children can:

- Bring you a book

- Fluff a pillow

- Wipe your face and hands with a towel

- Sing you a song

- Share a toy with you

- Get you a piece of fruit

Older children can:

- Fix window shades

- Bring cold water in an unbreakable container

- Make up simple foods such as cheese sandwiches, bowl of cold cereal, peanut butter on crackers

- Tell you a story

- Turn on radio, TV, etc.

- Make you a picture or get-well card

If you can't arrange for someone to help with the care of your child, you can have him play near you so you know he is allright and let him eat fruit, water, crackers—things he can get for himself. Perhaps he can find a big towel to put on the floor near your bed so you can both have naptime together.

Recycled Materials   Save things for rainy days, holidays, company days, lonely days, busy days, sick days, and all days. Keep a duffle bag in a closet or a box under a bed and store in it some old standbys a child can depend on and occasional "surprises" to spark the active imagination:

- Paper towel and toilet rollers
- Old decks of cards, complete or incomplete
- Foil containers, trays from TV dinners, pie plates
- Plastic storage containers and lids
- Greeting and Christmas cards
- Boxes of all sizes and shapes
- Used jar rings
- Empty spools
- Buttons
- Shoelaces
- Poker chips
- Elastics
- Styrofoam from packaging
- Yarns, ribbon, trimmings
- Lace doilies
- Plastic tomato boxes
- Popsicle sticks
- Cardboard liners
- Magazines
- Scraps of material
- Marbles
- Sponges
- Cotton balls, Q-tips
- Paper plates
- Egg cartons
- Straws

ALL ABOUT ME

"How come I'm so plain and you're so fancy?" a child asks a nude adult. Accept and encourage this curiosity. Answer as simply as possible. Sex education begins at birth, and joy with the natural body is observed at once. The patting and soothing of lotions and powders on infant skin is the first sensual experience. Cuddling, holding, and rocking extends this important intimate contact. A loved child will love. A touched child later gives of him or herself.

Long and complicated explanations for biological functions are usually more than a child is ready for in the early years!

The pregnant aunt had just gone home when the little boy suddenly asked his mother where the seed had gone. She brightened to this precocity, prepared to give first lessons in sex education. "Well, Uncle Max planted the seed in Aunt Elaine . . .," she began but he impatiently interrupted, "no, the seed I'm growing for my teacher, remember?"

Fascination with the human body is natural for people of any age. This is particularly true for the child who is trying to control bowels and urine, trying to adapt family health and safety rules to his own needs. Hot and cold, wet or dry, awake or sleepy, hungry or not, all of these are *physical* attributes often in conflict with his guardians. A child wears a sweater when his *mother* is chilly. A child also goes to bed when the parent is either tired or sick-and-tired.

Openings   Young children like to touch and explore their body parts. "So many 'openings' humans have," they may think. Since children know no "right" or "wrong," why should touching the genitals be "bad"? Explain that most body "holes," such as eyes, ears, nostrils, navel, etc. are delicate and need special consideration. When bathing a child, clean these areas gently. The child will immediately understand.

Wetting   The elimination functions are sometimes the most exasperating aspects of child raising. There are those who talk like professors and still wet, like the child who could request the kind of diaper he wanted to wear but was still wearing them!

And there are others who train early and easily. "Ready" is the key word here. Give praise for dryness. Criticism for "accidents"? Never!

Mirror, Mirror on the Wall   A necessary item in a child's room is a full-length mirror. The fascination of examining oneself reaches into old age. A child sees if he or she is getting taller, can make a muscle, can compare size to a sister, parent, sitter, etc.

Seasons   Children often regard parental attempts at dressing them properly as a mere nuisance. They may ask, "Why wear a sweater, raincoat, or rubbers?" Small children can't understand that shorts were allright yesterday, but changing weather means clothing changes as well. A calendar to remind them of changing seasons is an aid to parental nagging.

People   Point out physical characteristics when watching people: the old man with warts, jowels, fringe of hair on a bald pate; the old woman who is slightly bent; the pregnant woman and how she walks; and the noses, eyes, type of hair, etc. of the people watched.

Genetics   "Help me accept what I cannot change, change what can be changed, and to know the difference." This adage applies to physical characteristics as well as life's problems. A young child can learn about genes, the "magic" that makes blonde hair, freckles, long noses, dimples, etc. For example, point out that Susie and Daddy both have a curly hair gene, and that Grandpa and Buddy both have blue eyes, when everyone else in the family has brown ones. Such instruction later helps a child destined to be either the shortest or tallest member of the class. If hunching or stretching won't help, one may as well accept the genes one's forefathers have passed along.

Furniture   Adults are usually conscious of child-size furniture. Have you also considered eye-level hangings? Hang pictures and decorations lower than adults require. Move them up as a child grows!

**Just Like
Mom and Dad**
Nothing makes a child feel more grown-up than showering with a parent!

**Body...Rhythm
and Voice**

DANCE

on the grass
on the sand
in fields
on the pavement
in the house
    like a bird gliding
    like a bunny hopping
    like a deer running
    like a butterfly darting
    like a snake wiggling
    like a fish weaving
        in circles, holding hands
        with a partner
        in an adult's arms (such a lightfooted partner!)
        ALONE

SING

with the radio
with records or tapes
in the car
as you go for a walk
in the tub or shower
with someone
ALONE

Growing
Help your child with all his or her "growing pains" which mean growing up. Losing teeth signal the end of baby teeth and is a visible physical change for a child.

Motor coordination is rough and clumsy for the very young child and becomes more refined with maturity. Assure your child that not-staying-in-lines is unimportant and that as skill develops the fingers will have a better hold on the crayon. This applies to cutting with a scissors as well, a highly refined skill.

That desire to try on an adult's shoes are a symbolic reflection of every small child's yearning to be as big—and as powerful—as those who guide and protect him. Assure him or her that the longer the legs the more opportunity to run faster. Will he ever catch up? Should he even try?

And as this infinitesimal pattern of "catching up" takes place, the moments of childhood slip away like sand in the hour glass. No matter how difficult the days have been, ENJOY your child, for soon the small one will be full grown, leaving you only with memories of those early nurturing days.